The Untold History of Planet Earth

by

Michael E. Morgan

The Untold History of Planet Earth
Copyright © 2018 by Michael E. Morgan
All rights reserved. No part of this book may be reproduced
or transmitted in any form or by any means now known or to be invented,
electronic or mechanical, including photocopying, recording,
or by any information storage and retrieval system without written permission
from the author or publisher, except for the inclusion of brief quotations in a review.

Some of the material has been adapted from The Adventures of God, Copyright ©
2006, 2015 by Michael E. Morgan (Scottsdale, AZ: Dawntrader Books, 2015).
All biblical quotes are taken from the Holy Bible: New King James Version (New
York: Thomas Nelson Publishers, 1982.)

For information write to:
Dawntrader Books, LLC
PO Box D7-413
North Scottsdale Road
Scottsdale, Arizona 8266

If you are unable to order this book from your
local bookseller, or Amazon.com, you may order
directly from the publisher.
Quantity discounts for organizations are available.

Cover and book design by
Michael E. Morgan

Publisher's Cataloging-in-Publication Data
ISBN 9-7817322981-6-3
10 9 8 7 6 5 4 3 2 1

Contents

Introduction...4
CHAPTER 1: The Emergence...9
CHAPTER 2: A New Wrinkle..18
CHAPTER 3: Trouble in Paradise...26
CHAPTER 4: The Counsel of Nine...36
CHAPTER 5: The Judgment...44
CHAPTER 6: The Situation Worsens......................................48
CHAPTER 7: Luxcius's Plan...56
CHAPTER 8: Best Laid Plans...65
CHAPTER 9: The Defiance..73
CHAPTER 10: The Struggle Begins..80
CHAPTER 11: Plans Go Further Astray..................................92
CHAPTER 12: The Betrayal...104
CHAPTER 13: The Confrontation..112
CHAPTER 14: War Breaks Out...122
CHAPTER 15: The Truce..134
CHAPTER 16: Cold War of the Heart....................................141
CHAPTER 17: The Emissary...150
CHAPTER 18: Other Heavens, Other Earths........................180
CHAPTER 19: As Above, So Below......................................186
CHAPTER 20: Cycles Upon Cycles.......................................198
CHAPTER 21: The Law of Octaves......................................206
CHAPTER 22: Arcturian-Sirian Gambit.................................215
CHAPTER 23: The Alien Agenda..224
CHAPTER 24: The Limited Homo-Sapien.............................236
CHAPTER 25: The Cosmic Transformation..........................240
Epilogue..248
Glossary..252

Introduction

The Highest God, or the One Most High, chooses to speak through a human currently to make sure her plan remains on track. I believe this is the sign everyone is looking for. She has chosen to speak to us confirms this is a time of tribulation, but her contact also means we stand on the threshold of a miraculous turning point for humanity. Dark forces prevent any further understanding by creating confusion and doubt and causing a further entrenchment of our consciousness into the illusion on Earth.

The Untold History of Planet Earth is an adaptation and furthering of The Adventures of God. It reveals the nature of the Supreme Creator that has not been presented before. The Untold History shows the wonderful and most important aspects she has brought forth—unconditional love, compassion, and free will—which are represented through our basic nature as imprints from the fallen.

As animal hybrids hosting fallen imprints, we can raise our vibration to the level of the One Most High and resolve the issue of the fall. To accomplish this, we must learn the truth of the situation on Earth. By using our being to express love, compassion, and free will, we can extend her way to the lower realms.

I have always had an interest in spiritual subjects, and as a young man questioned everything. I was not satisfied with Church rhetoric and simple dogma. I wanted to know God personally. An opportunity arose years ago when a profound spiritual experience changed my life forever. After fasting, yoga, and meditation, I had a near death experience. I left my

Introduction

body and spent three days with the Highest God.

When I returned to my physical life, I denied the whole experience as a psychotic break from my fear of death and dying. But I remembered her warning; I would deny the experience. Later I would laugh at myself and cry about her wisdom. Then I realized the truth of this path. I was on my own, and I had to trust in the experience with her and make it real for myself without her help. This would make me strong and worthy of being of the highest realm.

Thirty-two years later, in bed one night, I felt peculiar and had trouble sleeping. I decided to use the breathing exercises I had learned to relax my mind and body. The room filled with bright light, a familiar and loving light. My body shook with energy as I saw and felt her again. The One Most High was nearby. Tears rolled down my cheeks like rivers. I was joyous to feel her so close. She greeted me warmly, caressed me like a child, and declared she wanted me to write her story.

I sobbed uncontrollably, so overcome with emotion I could not speak. I trembled and wondered whether I could accomplish such a momentous task. I felt her love and confidence penetrate me along with her friendship and trust. She reassured me not to worry. She would be with me the whole way to support me. And so, I began.

I wrote The Adventures of God. It was difficult but did not feel complete, but I was called and agreed. I have written The Untold History of Planet Earth with profound love, compassion, and devotion for the Highest God. The story is hers, but my part is a desire to convey a loving and compassionate Creator, a very personal God, who is my friend. She is the One Most High; other gods before her were controlling, jealous, vengeful, and self-serving without any unconditional loving kindness.

I am not a special person, but I did want to meet her above all else. In my experience, I learned that anyone could approach her as I managed to do, if they put her above all else. There is no need for an interceding influence. Let me prepare you for the greatest story you have ever read.

In the world of humanity, stories have the basics of a beginning and an end. Men and women want the comfort of knowing how something began as well as how it will end and prefer everyone lives happily ever after.

The spiritual realm here is different; the form is spherical. Boundaries expand into a finite zone and time moves in ever-increasing circles to fold back again. This leaves no straight path of marking the passage of events. No single sun divides the day from night or breaks a day into hours and minutes. Everything happens at once and then repeats.

Stories told about the adventures of humanity also define where the events unfold. This story does not have Earth in the beginning, although later it involves Earth very much. This story belongs to a region known as Heaven, which from the human perspective is upward.

Even as ancient scribes opened the book of Genesis with, "In the beginning," this story does also. I wish to keep the reader from the torture as to how it started.

There is not up or down, or left or right in Heaven. There is no specific point of beginning that we can understand. Since

Introduction

this is about the One Most High and Earth, it starts from a place of nothingness.

How do you tell a story from nothing? Nothing implies no one had observed the transition from nothing to something. The purpose of The Untold History is to bring understanding of this aspect, which goes beyond the finite and into the infinite. her emergence out of nothing is the first alchemical mystery.

The Holy Bible is the sacred text widely accepted as a spiritual record of prehistory on the planet and been translated into many languages. In truth, the Bible has been altered so many times to suit political and religious agendas it is hardly an accurate reflection of history. Genesis starts with, "In the beginning, God created the heavens and the earth." Some scholars read the passage as: "Those on high observed the heavens and the Earth." This is a very different perspective. It suggests that someone or something else existed at the same time as the Highest God. To tell the story of the One Most High requires an observer, known as "those on high" in this case. Without them, this adventure could not be told.

I do not seek to challenge the authenticity of any biblical translation, but rather consider other possibilities. It is also important to cross check and recognize those who have gone before. Many have labored with good intent to bring this important literature to the forefront that by every account appears to be a copy of records much older. The Hebrews made the Sumerian history texts their own, with their own names for the participants. This is different from what we have been told.

The intent of The Untold History is to circumvent political and religious agendas and describe the true history of the Highest God and begins well before the account in the Bible. The Adventures needed to be expanded to include more details about what happened in Heaven as well as the One's relationship to Earth. Her story is still happening. The Untold History serves as a tool to better understand the Creator and her ways, as well as the situation on Earth and the spiritual implications.

[Note to the reader:] The Highest God exists in a spiritual state beyond polarity. She possesses male and female properties and is androgynous, despite the God image on Earth that suggests a father in a male-dominated world.)

Many of the concepts presented may be foreign and shocking, but it is important for those who question the nature of this reality, The Untold History will function as a handbook to explain the unexplainable. It is a leap to embrace this book, but it will change your view of the world, the universe, and beyond. This is how her story begins.

The Emergence

In the time before time began, a place existed which could only be described as the void. The void is a dark place, but not in the sense humans know darkness. It would be more like the absence of light, or an absence of anything tangible or physical, for the physical universe had not yet manifested.

There were no stars, galaxies, planets, or moons. Deep within the vast dark regions of this primordial space existed several immortal races, God-like beings that knew no beginning or end. Since there was no time in this place, there is no way of knowing how old these beings were, or how they came into existence. Someone may wonder where they came from and perhaps how they came to be, but these mysteries stand unanswered at this point.

All that is known is they seem to emerge into existence as a response to the condition of the void. Difficult as it might be to imagine, the space itself becomes pregnant and gives birth to these creatures. So, they exist and have existed for all time as we know it.

The story must begin with one race known as the ancientDjinn, a vast number of immortals bound with a self-imposed construct of laws and structure providing a foundation for their existence. They are beings of energy and intelligence, a concept difficult to grasp. Usually, intelligence is attributed to something physical, like the brain in the human being.

Their world exists by virtue of their undivided view of a rigid control of their reality. They are emotionally neutral in human terms. There is a complete lack of emotional response. To grasp their perspective, the author developed a certain humanistic overlay of their responses, to enable the reader to grasp their approach to their reality. Their knowledge is immense though unique to their world.

As each one of their kind came into being, the group would identify them by the quality of the space and its traditions, and so named and confirmed them. Then they continue to exist within the group known as the collective. Their way of being, is defined by their control of their reality. That way is known as the way of dominion.

The collective recognized a potential energy appearing to move within and about the void and a standing wave of new consciousness pressed through but was not yet manifested. This was not unexpected, however. This region of the collective heaved and convulsed for an indeterminate period, perhaps even for a full eon.

The immortal energy of the Djinn collective always became supreme just before explosively manifesting. This is always a sign that the will of the collective will once again bring forth another one of its own kind, and it is now near reaching that point of emergence.

There is a strong sense of pride and excitement raging through most of the collective. One could perceive a distinct and palpable flood of telepathic exchange all around this zone. Not all are so inclined to be exuberant about this event. They considered this turbulent region the backwater zone of the void and known among the Djinn as the Archway of Praxxis.

The energy there is unpredictable and chaotic. The

The Emergence

consternation about this emergence is with the apparent peculiarity that a Djinn would arise there. Some have even dared to suggest that this emergence is spontaneous. They would consider this idea alone, among the collective, as blasphemous. Still, when an emergence is about to occur, despite any misgivings, the collective readjusts itself in a fateful way and yields to the outcome of its own nature. The area became more turbulent with a constant energetic froth arising out of the splashing of energy against energy, against certain greater densities in the void, very much like a series of oceanic waves crashing against a rocky cove. The maelstrom of impetuous light emerging in that place is like an awesome fountain of wonder.

It disturbs and becomes disruptive to be there for the Djinn. So, the Djinn would avoid that place. They defined it to be seductive against their way of control. This may seem strange that there was such a place within the realm of the Djinn. The Djinn's way is a strong, traditional and conservative framework of consistency within the collective, and the exact nature of the collective has not changed for eons upon eons. They have always known it as the way of dominion.

The area was fertile, brimming with the promise of something new and remarkable. The Djinn tried to ignore their instincts and rallied with a certain hope and with measured caution that something new and refreshing could come out of this region. Yet, they could not, or would not allow something non-traditional within their own ranks.

Anything unexpected, anything they could construe as

disruptive, would be unimaginable. Yet, among many of the High Council, there needed to be a strong belief festered, that something special could arise in this most chaotic of all realms. Some believed in the idea of 'fresh blood', if added to the mix of the collective, could be a most desirable event imaginable.

This new soul emergence suggested the collective reached an evolutionary breach. They could not embrace this disturbing aspect with an already well-established quadrant of the dominion. Speculation about the true nature of the effect of this new emergence, how it was to be channeled is the subject of many recent High Council meetings.

The moment had come when many members of the High Council, along with many delegates of other quadrants, formed a ring to surround the event horizon. The dark void heaved again and again under the influence of the standing wave now streaming forth from the new One. All was unfolding as expected. With each wavelet, the potential rose to capture and gather the space near it, compressing it, moving it toward the center of the event. The stress on the space in the surrounding area forced a spontaneous incline of those present, leaning inward toward the event center, and added to the remarkable focus of immortal energy.

Each wave recurring past those in the surrounding ring, caused a murmuring arising in unison, pressing forth like a chant over and over. The chant like prayer continued in each Djinn, as if to say.

"Stronger be the force of power, ring pass not this exalted tower, majestic sage to rule oblivion, by divine decree we grant dominion."

On and on the energy pressed. Folding back upon itself increasing again and again, gathering unto itself, a greater sense of all and everything, and with itself, an increased sense of the boundary growing dense now, while at the same time, shrinking smaller and smaller. The blinding light from the crushing force of space folded on itself and rushed toward its center, gobbling up all the space surrounding its core. The space collapsed like a giant avalanche of vortexes incavitation, rotating the void in and out of matter and anti-matter at a frightening pace.

Then, the light emitting from this amazing spectacle suspended itself as if frozen in an endless moment. The form, from the formless, stood shimmering in the night standing clear for all to see, a great crystal with many colored facets. The facets shimmered with a dazzling display, reflecting the light within and without.

The new One was complete. All was well with this quadrant of turmoil and chaos. The One had come within its midst to establish a new calm, a renewed structure, a renewed dominion ruling supreme over all that is here. The Dominion held all that is, secure within its framework of stability and assured constitution, a permanent and final solution to the chaos.

There seemed to be a sigh of relief as the ring of Djinn began to breakup, all greeting each other with a certain sense of pleasure and confidence, knowing all was well in their multi-verse. When they retreated into their own spheres and zones of reality, a wave of intense pressure burst forth from the crystalline One, standing in their midst. A sudden thunderclap exploded from the new form, followed with an outcry, as if a thousand trumpets blasted a mournful note all at once. This awesome utterance shocked those Djinn nearby. Never among all the Djinns, in all the eons of their eternal dominion, had they ever experienced this vibration. There is only one word describing this expressed energy… rebellion!

From the new One came an outburst spreading rampant throughout the dominion, like a brush fire driven by a high wind. A new and radiant light filled the dark space surrounding the One. It cast sharp shadows beyond those standing in its midst. They all turned in unison, as if by a cued synchrony, by some invisible force. Cracks formed along certain facets, letting forth brilliant blue and gold energy spewing more foreign vibrations, sending ripples of fear and loathing within those nearby. They were repulsed at its magnificence. The horrible tremors of this new force moved with greater power and radiance until the penetration reached members of the High Council. These tremors moved like shafts of broken glass blasting through their inner most fiber.

They rushed with great swiftness to the zone of chaos grasping the situation at first hand. To their horror, they clearly could see something going terribly wrong. The new One continued to go through another metamorphosis. No-one, in the collective could do anything except to observe the unfolding phenomenon. This wondrous event rumbled through the vast structure of the Djinn as an earthquake of monumental proportions, rattling the foundations of their stability.

Many uttered to themselves, as well as to others, what this could mean. Members of the High Council approached cautiously, aghast over what they saw. Those of the other quadrants looked at the ancient ones of the collective with desperation, longing for a settlement of this disturbance and hoping to restore the calm stability known to them for an eternity.

The danger was clear to the younger Djinns looking on with great horror. They saw the unsettled appearance of the ancient ones, without a distinct sense of any adequate and immediate solution to the debacle. Not unlike their younger brethren, the ancient ones stood by helpless to affect anything meaningful. They too awaited the eventual outcome of this disturbing and unpredictable event in their midst.

With every new change unfolding before them, gasps of horror and dread followed from the onlookers. Blinding light streamed forth from the new One, seeping from the fracturing crystal, too strong and painful to embrace. These bright rays were too bright for the dark velvet realms of the Djinn. Each in its own way split the darkness with a certain violent passion never experienced.

Changes kept coming, speeding up the metamorphosis exponentially before any of the ancients could grapple with the situation, offering no cogent response. Each new change presented by the new One brought more serious considerations, implying greater consequences for their influence upon the collective.

Meanwhile, deep within the core of the One, conscious awareness was multiplying and amplifying with an immense intensity. her passion focused upon an irresistible urge now growing within her being. A new intolerance emerging within her awareness, pressed against her form, defining her boundaries. This unusual aspect defined a sharp departure from ancient traditions normally found with the emerging Djinn collective. This singular difference pressed out from within her core, caused a blast of heat and light, not unlike a hot volcanic magma, building and increasing pressure against the boundary that contained her. There was only one burning thought, one burning passion, to be free, free of all boundaries, free of the form of ancient traditions that bred her.

With one final push, one final outcry of frustration regarding the intolerance to any limitations, she exploded in a violent eruption. Caring no longer for her existence, she surrendered and trusted to the purest evolution of her divine will, to be greater than all She is, or nothing at all! She sent her passion for freedom rushing outward through the dark void, past the ancient Djinns and the elders of the High Council. An increasing spherical envelope of spiritual substance and energy spewed forth, containing bright star clusters of concentrated intentionality, surrounded by swirling divine energies rotating about the centers of those clusters of pure consciousness, each embedded within finite aspects of her essence of divine freedom.

As the Djinn retreated from this magnificent display of insurrection to their traditional divine structure, the One expanded further her envelope of evolving expression of freedom. Thinking that this final explosion, would be like a candle burning twice as bright and lasting half as long, the elders retreated to their own realms to deliberate upon this ominous debacle.

At once they lodged charges against this abomination, claiming nothing calm or stable could have ever come out of that forsaken zone of chaos. Further, some wanted the zone declared as inviolate, a place where no Djinn should ever venture. Now, they gave little consideration about the fate of the One since they believed she exploded out of existence. The High Council could not comprehend what was happening. It is a true mystery unfolding within their midst, something inconceivable to them. They had given birth to a 'biological sport', an evolutionary mistake.

Hidden deep within their essence embedded the possibility their nature could regenerate into something that represents their compliment, their opposite. They were still to learn more of her evolutionary essence, still growing and well underway. They had yet to discover the full implications of this far-reaching confluence to their foundation, something beyond structure and without structure, embodying the purest energy free of form, the first formless Djinn.

The speed of the One's sphere of influence slowed, while the surface of her volume grew larger. The size of this volume could not be determined without the reference of time. So, space was indiscernible. To offer some spatial reference, we measure space by the speed at which light travels within one year. Hundreds of thousands of light years measured in parsecs could not define the boundary that was ever expanding.

There were countless starry clusters representing psychic nuclear points of her consciousness. Each of these clusters, like cells of the whole, all combined as the One's divine mind. Each point represented one Stellar Mind, each an individual spiritual aspect of her energetic form. There were a finite number of Stellar Minds, but the exact number was not known. Like the One's original energetic form, these new components possessed the same quality of the One's intent, expressing free will, but through their individual aspects and perspective.

Unlike those attributes of the Djinn collective rising beyond her, the witness aspect of the One's awareness existing as part but beyond the individual cluster cells. her will and purpose acted as an invisible binding force. her witness functioned as the supreme overseeing influence. This influence was a positive propulsive energy, not dissimilar to the male positive propulsive energy of the Djinn but appearing distinctly as the Divine Feminine. This prime mover, the Mother Goddess, instilled with a profound passion of joy and happiness, while ever creating and recreating herself, multiplying exponentially with each recurring wave of intention.

The expression to be all and everything at will, without limit, frightened the Djinn. False rumors spread while the outspoken complaints continued among the collective. They grew intolerant of her existence.

Each individual component of her crystallized being since her explosion, spawned numerous facets from the crystal and each of these facets of consciousness were called Stellar Minds. They all expressed her will intention, reflecting the One's unique light and love, like beacons projecting throughout her volume to the outermost fringe. The immense patterns of conscious energy within her system, were like neural networks, found inside the brain of a human being. They connected in a great unified family of neuronal-like synapses. Energy exchange occurring constantly with each, as they evolved into more complicated networks within the expansion of her increasing omniscient potential.

From the start, the Djinn did not describe the form of the One as wrong. It was more about their fear of something so different. her strangeness made them uncomfortable. They were not accustomed to her spontaneous and unpredictable energy disrupting the static balance throughout their realms. The collective turned to the elders for some definition of this phenomenon. They wanted answers and solutions to resolve this disturbance. They wanted to return to the peace and calm of the expected, the structure of controlled reality restored.

The most disturbing aspect of this event, from the point of view of the elders, was the clear dissolution of the One's form and core. They could not grasp the meaning and continued dispersal of her essence into countless secondary centers of influence called the Stellar Minds. To them, the One seemed to function more like a hive of spores, spreading like a virus among their kind. Second, the general lack of her focused presence appeared to the elders like an absentee host, or as the humans might put it, a ghost within her own shell.

The dominant feeling among the elders was strong for the need to stop the expansion of this foreign expression. Differing factions within the council, however, represented various points of view. Not all the Djinn were against this new phenomenon. Some were even hopeful of the outcome, waiting to see the result. Despite the forming of a loose alliance to the One's expression, most council elders continued to push for a final resolution.

They insisted that the new young Djinn showed, in her rogue expansion, a distinct cavalier disregard for traditional values instilled within the collective. They further advocated her presence may threaten the foundation of the collective, the way of dominion. Then, while in the middle of the furor, a new wrinkle appeared on the horizon.

In the world of the Djinn, the energy and expression of their light is always male propulsive. The Djinn light streamed forth out of each of their cores, in a constant and steady way. It was a quality, somewhat less, but not as vibrant, not as white hot as that of the One. Each were powerful in their own way, unique within their realms. Each realm, defined by its own separate vibration, each in its own sphere of influence, all existing within each other, like dimensional spheres within spheres.

Now, near the fringe of the One's expression, the positive propulsive blue and golden light streamed forth, but shifted in color. Something peculiar happened. The harmony and unity of consciousness from some Stellar Minds altered. The value of their light became strange, almost monochromatic, possessing an unusual singularity in their value.

A dull lack-luster quality eroded the dazzling appearance of her light, which first appeared so positive and alive. Something significant changed within some individual stellar clusters. A hesitation appeared in their movement, a distinct retardation in their individual will to expand.

The One, aware of all emerging within herself, did not react negatively to their shift. Within the framework of her new passionate paradigm, all freedom to express was good and righteous. The One took no interest to consider this alteration. To her, it was nothing more than a variation, a continued differentiation of her ever-expanding and evolving pattern of consciousness.

For the first time within the realm of the immortal Djinn, a feeling sense of true darkness emerged. It may sound strange to say, since their realm comprised the continuum of the dark void. This was different. There was a sense of polarity in the light that emerged. The shift of reality became harsher and more disruptive. The sense of freedom that expanded throughout their existence took on a shadowy and foreboding quality.

To be clear, this shift of light into dark, did not arise due to some doubt about the One's intentions. Among these Stellar Minds, it was a greater sense of curiosity to explore this new direction, the direction of contraction. They were innocent as to the implications of this new movement. They pursued this new direction with the same dedication, fervor and steadfastness that defined the overriding will of the One.

As most of the Stellar Minds continued to expand the golden- blue light of love and freedom of expression modeled by the One, the others explored something most peculiar, something new within their experience of themselves. They explored the opposite of expansion...the act of contraction. This movement was new and never witnessed by any immortal Djinn, which also included other immortal beings living in the vast dark void alongside the Djinn.

It was unheard of and unimaginable. The nature of this unusual contraction was simple. They didn't want to stop their part of the One's expansion, but rather to implode her expression in the opposite direction. Their will desire was to reduce their ever-increasing consciousness, all within the harmony of the One's realm. They eliminated their sensitivity to all and everything of the One, step by step. They wanted to observe and experience the process with all its effects.

To the One, this seemed plausible. The One considered the idea to be consistent with any concept of free expression, so long as there is joy and passion within the movement, their way of expressing her will, was sanctioned.

The elders of the High Council approached the One and inquired.

A New Wrinkle

"Have you given your 'word' for these individual parts to undertake this most unusual way to express?"

The One paused for a moment to reply.

"No. We have not given the 'word'! But do We need to? Is it not true and right that within the freedom to express, there is no need of the 'word' to approve or disapprove!"

The ancient Djinn of the High Council balked at her response.

"How can you dare to reject the ways of dominion? These are our ways, the ways of kindred immortals, the foundation of the collective, the only way possible and allowed! If you do not give your 'word', there will be disorder and chaos abounding!"

The One again paused before responding.

"What you say may be true within a bound structure. As you can witness, our movement is free of any kind of binding structure. A preordained structure requires an order to maintain itself. Our lack of structure allows the freedom to alter the form at will. This suggests a new way. In our way, if a need arises, let the one that feels drawn to fulfill the need respond to the need, on their own volition. Then, with this case there is no need to give our 'word'."

The elders backed away, aghast of the One's view on this matter.

They turned to assimilate her thought-forms. Then Bael, leader of the Elders of Old and Supreme Leader of the High Counsel, stood forth and proclaimed.

"What you say is blasphemy! Only disorder can come from

spontaneity. We can see no reason to this lack of responsibility in your manifestation. You must cease and desist with this movement at once!"

Again, the One took a moment to deliberate their thoughts. Then She went on.

"Is it not the primordial law, known beyond and recognized by the first of our kind; 'That which is undertaken, cannot be undone, for the primary cause set in motion, the effects are thee bound to?" The One smiled after this statement, knowing it would be an inescapable argument out of their own decree, and thus a supreme dilemma for the High Council.

Bael kneeled to speak more directly to the One.

"Be careful young one. In your cleverness to use the law, you may have sealed your fate. For is it not true also; 'That the absolute doctrine of the law governs all reality'. This defiant action on your part is seditious and lawless. These could warrant the Counsel's recommendation for the elimination of your expression. You have not been confirmed yet, young One! You would do well to yield to your elder's wisdom in this case. The wisdom to follow the elder's guidance is a fundamental requirement set down in the creeds of the Elder Djinn doctrine."

The One paused once more, before responding.

"Dear brothers, don't be upset with my movement. We are here to fulfill the law, not to break it! Why not let the cause we have set in motion, be evaluated by their results? The effects express the law, and we must experience it. If there be the need to judge Us for our expression, then let the Witness of the law unfold, what will be as well as, be the seal of Our fate."

Bael whirled around, to turning his back on the One with scorn. He motioned for the others to leave. Then he turned his attention once more to the One with a warning.

"This is not over yet young One. The time of your reckoning grows nigh. Your ways will not pass without the Sepulcher of Judgment. Let us see then how clever you'll be!"

In the central portion of the great regions of the One's expansion, a vast stellar mist swirled with varying brilliant hues of emerald, green. Then those colors succumbed to large soft reddish tones followed again by intense purple swaths bursting forth, pulsating in a marvelous dance of light.

The One could not help feeling a certain pleasure. The pleasure exuded from everywhere and invited an irresistible smile while she observed the immense shimmering surfaces ripple and unfurl from the wake of her invisible breath. Her vision of beauty and passion raced across the depths of the dark void like great interstellar sails not yet seen by any mortal eye.

Deep within the mists of the triune stream, two stellar minds exhibited distinct qualities from the original crystalline form of the One and they were first to emerge from the expansion. They emerged exploring their unique essence and expression while groping with a certain innocence in their movement.

As Pollux and Childra merged to greet amid their continuous expansion. Then an epiphany arose between them almost simultaneously.

In their amazement, they discovered there is they realized another way. Instead of exploring expansion in their expression, why not explore what it would be like to be less? Why not, instead, withdraw their grand passion for an outward movement, in exchange for an inner movement? Then explore, in that moment, what could happen?

Even the mere thought of this realization, at once, changed the quality of their light. The light pouring forth from them became less. This unusual effect became fascinating to them. They accomplished the unimaginable; they created for the first time a new quality of light in their midst.

This quality differed from the vast unlimited dark void surrounding them. This quality seemed palpable, at once present and discernable within their space. Yet, they could observe it, as though it were independent of their existence.

This was a new darkness, alluring, mysterious. This reduction caused a creation of something beyond them. It seemed separate somehow. Yet, it was coming from their inseparable quality of united expression.

"How could this be?" Childra inquired of Pollux.

Pollux seemed troubled and bewildered. There was no immediate answer forthcoming, as was always the case before. It was as if they had found an end to the unlimited realm of the all-knowing. They discovered a boundary they did not know existed. Did they create this new boundary? They both wondered. The incident also created something else. Now, there began an insatiable curiosity. For the first time, they could discern this amazing perception, with a slight amount of 'individual' perspective.

The new darkness moved beyond and away from them like a great shadowy wave, dimming the effervescence of the expanding light of the One, for all to witness. It displeased those witnessing this phenomenon about its presence. By now, all in the collective were aware of this strange and disturbing quality called 'darkness.'

As if the One's presence wasn't enough to deal with, there was a new substance not categorized, analyzed, or otherwise processed in any normal Djinn way. A dark beyond the dark void, the beginning of something dense and repulsive to the collective, as a quality reflecting everything they weren't. The experience represented a certain lack, something like nothingness, deadness, with a subtle and supreme touch of numbness. The mere consideration of it caused their spiritual hackles to rise.

Polarity was unknown in the worlds of the Djinn. They knew only an expression of their consciousness as a singularity of light. They could only describe this new darkness as the absence of consciousness. The horror of this foreign substance brought a whole new fear experience to the collective, an immortal sense of xenophobia. This new palpable substance approached them, posing a genuine threat to conscious existence within the collective.

In the meantime, the other Stellar Minds in the near vicinity of Pollux and Childra looked on with bewilderment. Several drew near to comprehend this new experience of darkness, along with the underlying causes of the strange phenomenon coming forth from their brothers.

In the human experience, when siblings within the family group become distant with each other, a psychic separation is generated within the energy fabric of the family, a knowing that something has gone awry. The family instinct declares the family structure is in trouble. When the family feels a separation, or a loss of the connectedness within the group, the individuals of the family draw together to resolve, if possible, the issues causing the rift.

Here too, the other Stellar Minds approached their brothers to offer help and compassion for the separation that occurred. What they discovered surprised them. They expected some stress or anguish in the situation, but there was none. This stimulated curiosity from the others, forcing a deeper telepathic empathy with Pollux and Childra.

As much as the incident caused great anguish with the Djinn, there was also a powerful reaction from some of the other Stellar Minds. In an act of love and compassion, they too wanted to understand their brother's discovery of contraction. This act was not a collusion to reduce consciousness, but a desire to help and support Pollux and Childra. However, the incident is noted in some of the fragmented human records of ancient spiritual events, describing a grand conspiracy against the One.

In their attempts to comprehend this darkness, others added to the darkness and thus multiplied the phenomenon. The situation grew worse with every moment of their experience. It seemed an inescapable cause set in motion, and in unison, through the combined mental and emotional components of divine imaging, these Stellar Minds, together with their combined consciousness, brought into existence a primary First Cause, a lower vibratory plane of consciousness, less than the whole of the One. This became known as the Causal plane.

In the limited view of human experience, classified this emergence of lesser consciousness out of greater consciousness, as something evil. In the realm of the One, however, it was only a different way to express her life, as an experiment of reduced life. This expression seemed necessary and allowed in the realm of the One.

In the same way, perhaps in a democracy, where freedom of speech exists, that freedom must also allow for the talk of revolt or sedition against a nation's foundation, which is conceived of such freedoms.

Perhaps, in retrospect, this might have been the event referred to in the Genesis chapter, from the Old Testament, paraphrased as "The light cleaved from the light until there was light and dark".

Andrais and Ardenax, Stellar Minds representing courage and steadfastness within the origins of the One, examined the new Causal Plane of consciousness. They declared this was a perfect example of absolute freedom. This movement of decline, they argued, should carry on further, suggesting this variation on the theme of the One, warranted serious further experimentation and exploration.

They explained the experience of the Causal existence with a simple sense of presence, another state of being. This possibility exists because there was no sense of three-dimensional space. Meaning, if someone were in a room with a friend, enjoying an exchange of conversation of mutual contact, then left the room to enter another adjacent room, there could still be communication with the friend in the original room.

There would not be the same close quarter contact as being in the same room, but communication could continue. No sense of paranoia or alarm would arise in this case. The sense of trust from this distancing would not represent a deliberate attempt on the first one's part to separate from the other.

So, it was with those who discovered this reduction of consciousness. It seemed harmless and non-threatening. From the observer's point of view, it seems sad these Stellar Minds could not expect the ultimate ramifications of their combined movement.

Perhaps the total identification of their experimentation

became the true source of their separation from unity consciousness. So, they were helpless to continue blinded by their curiosity, pushing further into a deeper separation and polarity, intrigued by the effect of reducing their being into something realizably felt.

Perhaps, it is also important to point out, before the development of the Causal Plane of existence, nothing in the way of a physical universe existed yet. The light of Stellar Minds from the One and the light of the Ancient Djinn are not stars, nebula, or any other stellar objects in the night sky. Perhaps, it is important also to note, after the physical universe emerged, containing the aforementioned objects, the ancient ones of the Djinn collective, coexisted and cohabited within and about these starry apparitions within their own regions, defined by their unique vibrations of existence and being-ness.

It was Casiel the greater, Meluziel and Saganagral, which brought this process down to the next level of existence. It intoxicated them with some invisible spiritual narcotic. They absorbed and shared the new perceptions of degradation with ease and equal anticipation. They moved downward with a rush of discovery and surprise. The dramatic effects of each reduction remained mesmerizing.

With each new discovery brought excitement, however, a slight twinge of regret loomed over the adventurous spirits. There were unexplainable feelings arising for the first time. These spirits experienced longing, sadness, and a subtle sense of loss in orientation. What they took for granted, with their poise and sense of spiritual direction of the One, now seemed beyond their reach?

The One was still present, meaning they could remember her and her essence, but no longer any direct or indirect contact with her, or with any of the others still in the ascension and expansion of her realm.

Still, they continued, despite their growing sense of isolation, assured that this effect was only temporary, and could be reversed, should they choose to do so? They were divine immortal beings with free will. They believed in the freedom to explore in both directions.

The situation of this new direction grew more deleterious. These bold spiritual explorers stretched their will, reducing further their consciousness stage by stage, with each exhalation of their vital force. They expanded downward, contracting deeper and further than before.

From their first separation, an unwitting but certain letting go of the divine Mother binding them to the energetic fabric of the One, caused the fabric to heave and swell, giving birth to their departure. With each stage, from the whole of the One, descending into the first Cause, the 'Be-Cause' or 'Causal level' re-emerged in a denser state. It was the One's essence, of energy, form and witness collapsing into those regions of the falling Stellar Minds, lowering to an essence of imagination, awareness and will.

Then, with the next in-breath of the fallen ones, the density broke up into several polarized aspects, in a downward expansion defining the next lower level of existence, formed for the first time. This new lower level of existence is called the Etheric Plane. This awareness of the fallen reduced further into greater density and then fractured. The fracture dissolved into three separate parts.

These bipolar opposites exhibited both male and female qualities, representing an active principle and a passive principle. In the first of these three aspects of the Causal metamorphosis, a lower form of passive conscious 'awareness' was coupled to its shadow side of active 'understanding'. Then, in the second of the three aspects, 'imagination' dissolves into its bipolar opposite of 'insight', the active lower principle, and its shadow side of 'wisdom'. In the last of the three causal aspects, the lower 'will' now expresses as an active 'expansion' along with its shadow side of 'concentration'.

These new expressions of etheric existence led the fallen further away from the whole of the One. Increasingly, other Stellar Minds joined the original group, mesmerized by the fascination of the dark light they produced. The experience seemed exotic and tranquil. They found a strange solace in the clear sensation that active, vibrant consciousness didn't seem satisfying. This new consciousness was sanguine, without responsibility and narcotic, promising new pleasures apart from anything else that the One offered with her loving fabric of consciousness.

Though it was not yet clear to them, the fallen leaned away from the desirable support of the whole, moving steadily toward independent thought and expression, a heretofore unheard-of concept, shared only by those within the inner circle of the fallen.

Then, one stood before them, whirling his being in a wound column of misty vapor shown with the deepest red and burgundy. His prideful glare penetrated the others with disdain. He began a hideous laugh that was both mocking and impish. He moved back and forth before them, like an impatient father waiting for his first-born offspring.

Then he spoke.

"You don't get it do you?" he taunted. "All this searching, experimenting and exploring and it's as plain to see, as it would be for a child-ling. We set the course, the way is clear, yet you hesitate! Why?"

Childra stepped forward, concerned and confused.

"Whatever do you mean, brother Beleth? We have all labored to understand this manifestation with all our combined will and divination. Troubled that the reduction doesn't lead us anywhere, many of us feel we have failed the One, trying to express her complete free will… But this movement doesn't seem to lead us to any worthwhile conclusion!"

With his back turned, Beleth grimaced.

"My dear brother Childra," he said, while turning to face them all.

"You're intelligent. Your powers of divination are better than most, yet your foolish devotion blinds you to the misguided prophet of freedom. The One is making this up as she goes. I said it. The One stumbled onto this profound truth you've uncovered by accident!"

The rest laughed loud at the ridiculous inference of something accidental within the realm of the Djinn.

Pollux raised his vision from a bow of disappointment.

"Beleth, it's over. We've gone as far as we can go. We must return now to inform the One. This line of decline leads to nothing…worse, it leads us all into shame."

Beleth turned.

"I cannot believe my senses! You stand on the brink of

something monumental, and now you want to turn your backsides away, cowering before what you have done like some slithering thing? My friends. Do not stop now! You must follow through with what you have started. You owe the One that much, don't you?"

His vision bore down on them as daggers to a target. Beleth refused to let up his intent to goat them on. In what Beleth believed to be their greatest hour, the only recourse was to finish the work of absolute divine defiance. He focused his will upon his essence of fortitude. Like a great spear, he plunged it into their core. Thus, he cauterized their wounds of shame and hardened their cores. So, they pushed on to the ultimate sacrifice.

With one last thrust, another level of being-ness manifested. Now, from the Etheric, the lighter and delicate qualities of imagination, higher awareness and softer will would exude a darker level, with a hellish blast of exhalation. They fused together, developing a combination of denser energy, formed in the crucible of defiance. With a focused and determined lower will to exist, beyond the will of the One, it seethed a negative intellect, pure independent reason which would reckon with the One. The Mental Plane would allow them to deal on their own terms. The One's realm, challenged by the combined downward movement, took on heavier substance. Its name was rebellion.

The Counsel of 9

The most ancient of the Elders, Bael, Beliel and Arjaxx returned to the collective hall of justice for a meet with the High Council. The place of the High Council appeared like a Greek amphitheater. Perhaps the Greeks, inspired by this arrangement, with their intuitive take on the 'right' form to gather.

The moment came to deliberate on the One. The High Council formed when considering important matters. A crescent-shaped bowl with the Eldest at the bottom, the youngest near the top, creating a parabolic focus of the energy present. Their focus, toward the arena, or as the Djinn refer to it: The Platform of the Just.

When judgments get handed down, the form changes to a 12-member panel with a three-tier cluster of six-sided crystalline forms. The three Eldest sit a row on top. Those descend in order of position in the second tier of four. At the bottom tier of 5, are the youngest of the group. Discussion about the issue was already underway. Many side groups huddled, arguing the points with many heated exchanges.

They lingered on one singular point; one of their own, could emerge in such a chaotic place as the Archway of Praxxis. The shock of this still rippled through the collective. It represented a widespread catharsis. The centrifuge of anger fueled most of the complaints. It became the center stage for many outbursts at the meeting.

Tago, the lesser, spoke first, exclaiming.

"I think I can speak for many here. We want to know why there is an abomination rising in our midst? Why are you, our leaders, not doing something about it?"

Beliel stood to respond.

"To our brother Tago, we recognize his enthusiasm on this issue. We must contemplate these matters. Being younger, impatient and rushing into brashly made conclusions would add to the pattern, perhaps even add more to the chaos already present within our realms."

Saixx, sitting next to Tago, jumped to Tago's defense and declared.

"Well, I believe we mutually feel Tago's concern and the urgency. How long before we shall see action on this matter? Every moment that lingers, something more occurs with this thing growing like a tumor among us. Do you not feel that this kind of change is dangerous?"

Bael now stood beside Beliel to show unified support in the wisdom put forth by his ancient brother.

"Brothers, this is not a moment to divide in our purpose. We agree that this is of the utmost urgency and yet we must weigh all the evidence."

Three now stood representing the Ursa Major Quadrant, Anodon, Arinax the Bold, and Deloi the Just, pausing for a moment to allow the noise and heated clamor to subside.

"We of the Council of Nine bid a moment to offer a different point of view to consider."

Deloi continued.

"Brothers of the Council of the great collective, we are strong in our presence and need not fear this new One."

Grumbling and dispute began again, spawned by Haboro.

"What say you Deloi? Your clan is from the outreaches. What have you to offer to us? We hear your voice, but it is small, and has no meaning!"

Beliel answered to this heckling.

"Haboro, we must exhibit patience and allow all our brothers to make all points. We must never question later an issue and conclusions drawn. We must be sure it does not construe this meeting as ill-conceived, or worse, an illegitimate suppression of one of our own, by deliberate intention. Please continue, brother Deloi from the Ursa Clan."

Deloi returned.

"Thank you, Elder Beliel, for your support. We feel that this represents an important transition for the Collective. We recognize the overwhelming importance of tradition. So, do not misunderstand our meaning here. Many have had questions about the survival of the collective for many eons, whether they want to admit it! We believe the disturbance is meaningful because the new One has reflected our underlying consideration for ways to insure our continuation. More, that it remains strong, or becomes stronger."

Anadon chimed in.

"Yes. Brothers, and hail to the great and wise ancient ones who lead us through these treacherous waters."

Beliel responded.

"Yes, brother Anadon what say you here?"

Anadon continued.

"We are not here to sow the seeds of ill content, but to reveal something within each of us. Like it or not, our newest and youngest brother is so showing us perhaps some new way." More grumbling rises in response to the strong words of Anadon.

Malachais reaches forward from where he remained, still sitting, with a grimace of sharp disapproval.

"And you, young one, also have the audacity to proclaim

The Counsel of 9

yourself aged with enough wisdom to cast judgment on the collective's Dominion Creed?"

Anadon turns to face Malachias.

"The fact that her coming stirred us to such malfeasance shows weakness in our structure. It suggests the dominion needs our support, from a new perspective, if not a readjustment." More grumbling and argument between many members raised the noise to a deafening roar.

Bael raised his staff, bringing it down to the floor of the great Hall of Justice, causing a thunderclap. Only the Eldest of Djinn carry the Jaram Scepter. It is both a symbol and an artifact of great power and authority. Powerful waves of interesting force rippled out to the Djinn. Then the Hall became silent at once.

Bael followed.

"Brothers, let us be an example of calm and order here."

Now Arinax joined his brothers.

"Brothers of the great Hall of Justice, is it not true that our strength flows from the great Maoi, the primordial energy vibration of all, between us?"

A great sigh of acknowledgment rose in a unified groan from the audience.

Arinax continued.

"Is it not also true? We must prevail by not allowing the Maoi to become stiff to move. I beckon you to remember the noble words set down in our ancient records by the first Djinn; That which moves all is Maoi, and that which preserves Maoi shall also move all with it, or all shall perish in the remnants of its passing. So, let our youngest deliver us from the stiff way and restore the nimbleness of the great Maoi."

This brought many rumors and whisperings among those in the audience. There seemed to be a long pause that kept lingering, showing no reply to this. But the Elders did not want to leave the great Hall on a somber note.

Then Anadon added.

"On this point, the new One's vitality is without question. One must observe the quickness to which the new One can expand, like no other before us. We could learn from this One, even though she is the youngest among us."

Demiel, one Djinn of the Anasa Quadrant, reiterated the issues.

"We have listened to the Ursa Clan and hold these views self-evident, with respect. But I tell you, many things about the new One, warrants closer scrutiny. What of this dark substance she manifests? Could it not be a cloaking mandrel, hiding from us her true intention? Isn't this breaking the rule of the 'first directive': Thou shalt not hold separate thyself from the whole?"

Thus, she does not blend with us, not even from her emergence. Beliel admitted her defiance of the Elders and manipulated the law to defend her actions. Further, why does She segregate herself into many, while She hides beyond her own boundary? Does this not suggest something of a sinister agenda? What if she intends to multiply herself, through these altered cores, to launch a siege upon us all?"

A voice cries out from the audience.

"Is this true, Beliel? What say you to these claims?"

Beliel turned to Bael, then dropped his gaze to the floor momentarily. Then he spoke.

"I am cautious to lay accusations against a brother if she is new among us. By her lack of experience warrants leeway. It pains me to say, it is true! I have observed, the young one is provocative by her actions. I declare that the law should judge her."

Bael stood before the exceptional body of immortals and brought down his staff twice to the Hall floor. With resounding authority, he spoke.

"We cannot assimilate these deliberations without some input from the young One. Summon her at once! We shall discern for ourselves this provocative nature. Perhaps then determine her fate from her machinations."

The One responded to the summons without delay. She appeared on the Platform of the Just with a flash of blue light. She smiled upon the august body seated before her.

The Hall became silent while they gazed upon her with wonder and bewilderment.

Bael turned to the youngest of the collective with surprising patience, pleading.

"Young One from the Arch of Praxxis, it is not without grave concern we have summoned you within our presence. We have heard from many in the council about your actions. There are many allegations made against you. We Elders among the Council want you to respond and defend these actions."

The One still smiling at them, nodded.

"Dear brothers, of this most auspicious gathering of the supreme collective. We feel honored and pleased to stand before you. We look forward to answering all your inquiries."

Malachais stood up and jeered.

"There! You, see? Why do you not honor us with only the One, your core? What are these 'We' you refer to?"

The One, still smiling, responded.

"We are One, but We express as many, each with their particular perspective, all equal in their place within the whole, without hierarchy, but allegiant to the purpose of our will."

The audience expressed a gasp of astonishment at this remark. Haboro raised another question to the One.

"How can there be existence without hierarchy within your core? Is not this a pure example of your defiance of the way of dominion? For is it not known, the way of dominion is always from the order and structure of hierarchy, since the dawn of the first Djinn?"

The One stood. her words reflected an absolute assurance in her approach to her way of existence. She continued to respond to Haboro.

"We all share in mutual responsibility for matters of interest, with equal status. As a need might arise within the whole, any of the whole that is most aligned to the matter at hand responds with complete love and compassion to the matter. Therefore, no need for a decree is required to say which, of the whole, will do this, or do that."

The audience again reared back with a gasp of surprise at her remarks.

Beliel stared upon the One with intense focus, seeking an opportunity to trap her with his question.

"So, you admit to delegating your authority to these separate parts without regard to their independent direction. You do this, under a veil of secrecy, behind your wall of darkness? With this wall of darkness, do you have another hidden agenda? You have expressed a desire to change everything. Perhaps you seek to undermine, or even overthrow, the collective foundation? What say you to this claim, defiant one?"

The One turned serious with this charge. She turned, peering at Beliel as well as the rest of the Council before responding.

"Brothers, you mistrust Our way. You ask these questions with greater suspicion. Yet, we assure you, we mean no harm to you or the collective. We only seek to reflect on a new way to express the law, which would invite trust, unconditional love, and greater mobility with the great Maoi. We seek to strengthen the collective through relaxing the structure, suggesting a looser approach, with greater freedom of expression."

"Our clear separation from the whole of the collective is only that Our way is not confirmed. We need continued development before merging with the whole."

"As to the 'darkness' which has emerged within our form, we can only say, is a byproduct of the freedom of expression. When something new begins, you can expect it."

Bael reached forward to stop Beliel in another round of questions. He stood to raise his staff once more, letting it fall again to the floor, with a thunderous noise. Then he followed.

"Well. The most ancient Elders have heard enough. We declare these proceedings closed. We shall retire to deliberate on the evidence presented."

Bael turned to the One and spoke.

"You are free to return to your realm for now until there is judgment."

The One smiled, with a nod of acknowledgment.

Beliel turned to Bael, looking for out his inner reactions to the proceedings.

"So, what are your conclusions regarding the young one?" Bael appeared concerned.

"Yes. The matter is troublesome. It will require careful consideration because there is not the unity in this matter I had hoped for. There are many dissenters. That makes the situation more complicated."

Beliel responded.

"I thought the platform for her dissolution was clear! There is more than enough of a quorum for this decision, Bael. You need not worry about this, brother."

Bael turned to respond.

"You are impatient on this and assume it is well to proceed, but I'm not so sure. her dissolution may not be the best solution. What you suggest will satisfy the needs for the moment. But what if another of her kind arises? I'm looking for something to serve here as a permanent assessment of the effects and long-term resolution to the matter. It will set a benchmark for any which could arise later."

Beliel approached Bael with a sense of reassurance.

"Bael, I think you are far too concerned with this one. She is a freak of nature, one of a kind, and reckoned with. In this way, you can bring order back to the collective and thus r eaffirm your leadership as the Grand Elder of the Council. This will give assurance of your continuation in this role."

Bael answered.

"Beliel, if I didn't know better, I would say you have just informed me that my leadership is in question. Do you also seek after my position, Brother?"

The Judgement

Beliel bowed his head and dropped to the floor in the posture of obedience.

"Bael will forgive me for being presumptive and insolent." Bael demanded.

"Get up, brother. You look ridiculous prostrating before me!" Belial continued while rising.

"There has been talk…"

Bael looked at Beliel. "Yes… what talk?"

Beliel continued.

"Yes…. I do not wish to speak out of turn here, but yes… of your delay in handling this matter… but you must know it is not my perspective, brother. I have the highest regard for your ability to lead the Council."

Bael looked on.

"I tell you, brother; we must move here. The solution must serve us all. It must be broader in its application and will unite us once again."

Beliel seemed disappointed with his elder brother's hesitation to act.

"Brother, your wisdom will prevail, as always." Bael's expression turned abrupt.

"Leave me now, for I must consider this in the silence." Beliel already retreating, said.

"By your command, Elder."

The members of the High Court reformed for the passing of judgment. Bael, Beliel and Arjaxx sat at the top tier. They summoned the One. Once again, he appeared in a flash of blue light. There was nothing to discuss or deliberate, for now judgment is being passed down for all to witness. The Council sat before the Tier of Judgment to hear the decrees set down.

Beliel spoke first.

"Brothers of the Council, and known for all, the Elders and their brethren of the Judgment have deliberated upon the matter of this young one's case before us. They have reached a verdict that will stand unchallenged before the entire collective."

"Hear now the judgment."

The Hall of Justice was quiet, and the atmosphere seemed to tingle with anticipation as to the outcome. The One seemed relaxed, but alert, knowing that her fate as a Djinn in the world of Djinns was hanging in the balance.

Bael reached out through the blackness of the dark void with his utterance. The void shook with his vibration.

"Brothers of the Council, and all within the collective, from now in this moment and beyond the eternal, they shall deem the new One confirmed as a Djinn of the 9th order. She shall reign within her own sphere of influence, defined by the highest of her vibration. Yet, she and all her kind within the One shall be separate from the rest of the collective."

"Further, no Djinn of any other realm shall enter her realm unless invited by the One. We give her a free choice to continue her expressions without disruption from any other as she deems fit."

"For all known, Bael continued, that this does not make up a condoning of the One's actions. Her realm shall stand as an example for all to witness. We condemn this way of freedom by the court and shall disallow it within the collective at large."

"Nor shall the One try to incorporate her way into the collective and all its realms.

This is the decree of the elders of the High Court."

Bael then dropped his staff to the great hall floor three times and spoke.

"So, let it be said, so let it be done!"

"From this moment on, the One will be known as the nameless One."

"There is no recognized tradition to assert her name. We banish her from the collective and all its boundaries. There will be, henceforth, no contact made with the nameless One by any other and, if so, at their peril."

Bael dropped his staff again to the floor of the Great Hall three times, saying.

"So, let be said, so let it be done!"

The Situation Worsens

Deep within the outer regions of the One, Beleth, Casiel and Saganagra exchanged discussions with growing dissent. Beleth continued with his grumbling.

"Brother Casiel, do you not feel this new freedom? It's not like any experience we have ever felt before. This new perspective is fresh and without burden."

Casiel pondered Beleth's remarks and became puzzled. Then he responded.

"What do you mean, brother? Where is there a burden?"

Beleth continued to argue.

"Why! The burden of the overbearing pressure from the One. It's always her will, isn't it? Why then cannot there be complete freedom?" Beleth went on.

Saganagra chimed in.

"But we are also her freedom, we express in this way, isn't that freedom?"

Beleth jumped down to a lower level from where he sat.

"Yes, brothers, but are we free? Meaning, we are free to agree, yes, but are we free not to agree? Let us examine for a moment what we are doing here. We are choosing to contract. So, we are reversing the movement. Yes? And that I think is the real freedom! But that is also the problem!"

Casiel and Saganagra looked upon Beleth with a furrowed brow.

Then Casiel looked at Saganagra, shaking his head.

"We don't understand, brother. What are you saying?"

Beleth looked down with disappointment, now shaking his head.

He paused for a moment, thinking he might explode with anger. His brothers seemed to have lost their minds. Then he

The Situation Worsens

started again.

"Okay. Now try to stay with me on this. Look what we have created. We are standing here with our own mind, our own perspective. Why don't we use it? I know in my heart it would be what she would want for us… yes? What I'm advocating here is, it is the time we free ourselves from the One's tyranny of kindness. She sets us free, but we are not free."

Saganagra stared at Beleth.

"And what would this new freedom look like?"

Beleth placed his hand upon Saganagra's shoulder and responded.

"Well, we could agree together, to not agree! Then the One could not ignore that her way cannot be the only way!"

Beleth, still trying to convince Casiel, turned to face him.

"You tell me brother, how is she different from the other Djinns? She declares freedom but behaves as they do. Don't you see this, Casiel?"

Casiel looked down.

"I suppose you are right, brother. But what shall we do? It seems the only way now is to return to the whole and expand as the others do."

Beleth, assured now, he has forged new comrades, affirmed his alliance, and pushed them on.

"No! Brothers, this is our chance… maybe our only chance to show to the One we are standing up, following our passion as the One does, not retiring, not regretting to push on to a perfect conclusion."

"Now we must choose our way! We must carve out of her reality a slice of our own existence. Let us shift again, to reduce further our contractions until there is no further level to confirm our reality. We should declare our way to all and call our other brothers to align with our way. Why not band together? Let's declare that we refuse to go back to her way, then build our own realm separate from her. Then, we will be free… free to reign over our own kingdoms, doing our will and not her will!"

In time, many Stellar Minds followed Beleth's cry for greater freedom, though they did not yet realize the implications, or the result. Now the contraction that began with simple curiosity, conceived, and carried out, in the name of the One's will, descended into the deeper darkness of dissent and deliberate rebellion against the One.

They banded together with Beleth leading the way. With fervor and dedication, they marched into the darkness of unconsciousness to further reduce their awareness of anything except their own blind will, to be something different and separate, apart from the One, no matter what the cost.

Once again, they inhaled their pride and self-importance, brought on by their new mental body of independent consciousness, only then to exhale downward into a chaotic blast of lower conscious parts. Thus, the Emotional Plane emerged.

Now the dense material of their mental bodies exploded into five polarized aspects of positive and negative emotional energy. All the neutral and unconditional energy remnants of the One separated. It was like a crash of broken glass into the density they created.

It split these off sub-impressions like chards of the original, mere empty reflections of the divine vessel of passion from the One. These energies did not connect to any reality at all,

The Situation Worsens

but loose ephemeral copies of what was once, perfect harmony and grace.

The sad aspect of this dilemma, what they sacrificed, could not be remember. They lost all in the oblivion of darkness. The fallen ones could not appreciate their sorrow. From the loss at the beginning, they had no recollection of giving it up.

Then the Emotional body seemed to reform into clustered groupings of the densest material and as an unnatural evolution unfolded, the deepest most dense region of their creation, was the Astral Plane. It was like residue dripping from their explosion. Now their movement had come to a complete halt. At this level, they lost all genuine sense of vitality and motion. Yet, they didn't realize the genuine sense of their predicament.

They entered a dream. Their conceived reality where their imagination and mental capacities were engaged to maintain a non-real world, a physical matrix of density, a complete universe unfolded as reflections of a memory marred by separation, a poor replica of a grander place they once knew; myriads of stars, galaxy clusters with planets and moons, as vast as the realm whence they came.

The dream, conceived in their minds, came with extremely lucid details of their innermost fantasies and lost desires. This was the grand illusion of the first order, a complete realm created by them, where they didn't feel the loss, the sorrow, or the pain of their actions at first. But then, in this realm, they created time and space. Their dream turned into a nightmare of suffering and loneliness. Time emerged to reflect on their loss. Space emerged to reflect the immensity of their separation.

They did not realize this truth. They were so unconscious of what they were. These poor creatures, now just mere shadows of themselves, could not remember how to return home, even if they had wanted, now they could not.

The fallen, now completely lost. There was no workable way back to the neutrality of the One. Their polarity drove their beliefs, which reinforced their illusions. These Stellar Minds came to believe in the physical world they created, forgetting all about their intentions, their memory of the One, and of their intimate connection to her. It was as if they had gone off with their addiction of contraction, now they were ill from it.

The One grew concerned about their plight because she felt this strange energy of sadness, of loneliness and suffering. It was strange to her because it was not familiar with her realm of love, harmony, and joy. She realized that something was wrong and wondered how to resolve this horrible catastrophe.

Though She did not foresee this unfortunate outcome from their actions, she felt there was hope they could recover from this strange malediction. She knew her children were now lost. They needed help to find their way home. She felt no judgment about their attitude or their rejection of her ways. They directly attributed this awful condition to their sickness. Like a loving mother to wayward children, she beckoned them to come home. The great awareness within her reached out with her love and compassion, calling out to all those who had not fallen, hoping that one or more could come to the aid of their brothers.

The brightest and wisest of all Stellar Minds, Luxcius, stepped forward to where the One lived. He acknowledged the plight of his brothers and expressed his deepest sympathy with a certain understanding of the problem, as well as the urgency.

The Situation Worsens

Then he proclaimed.

"Oh, mother of us all, it is of the utmost importance we return these fallen ones back to the fold. Is it not also in our greatest interest to prove the Ancient Collective is wrong about your way of freedom?"

The One spoke.

"Dear friend, my right most trusted one. It gives me pleasure to see your concern and caring for your brothers. Yet, I hasten to add, it is not for my sake you do this, but for their sake."

Luxcius responded.

"Oh yes, mother, you are right. This situation is the gravest. With careful consideration proves most difficult and complicated. They must return with some honor and righteousness yet redressed of their trespasses against you."

The One again responded.

"So, what have you to say about this disturbing situation?"

Luxcius went on.

"After careful consideration, mother, I have deemed they need loving guidance from your eminence. Yet, while entrenched in their illusion, they must come to understand what they have done and learn from it."

The One said.

"Interesting. So, go on."

Luxcius continued.

"Well, what I have conceived is radical in approach. It will require your sanction."

The One responded.

"Yes. Well, my son, please continue."

Luxcius explains.

"I believe what we need to do is provide an arena where

they may continue with their illusions, but under controlled conditions. With your emanations provided, assist them to learn how to unlearn their ways of separation and relearn the way of union."

The One interrupted Luxcius.

"We don't see how this requires any special dispensation?"

Luxcius then explained further his plan.

"Yes mother, but this requires that we use one of their illusory worlds, a planet like they have conceived, except the planet is derived from us. Thus, through this action, we can embed within that world a path of light out of their worlds of darkness."

The One again interrupted.

"And how do you propose to accomplish this, when their worlds are dead to us?"

Luxcius responded.

"Yes, mother, but that's just it. We will need a volunteer to become such a world through the de-vitalization of his being on a living planet."

The One stood up.

"You mean to threaten another of my children through de- vitalization?"

Luxcius beckoned the One, to grasp his plan with patience.

"Yes, but it would be with our conscious control. With careful treatment, it lost nothing for the volunteer or the others."

The One paced back and forth, deliberating Luxcius's plan.

"And my son, who shall be this volunteer you have suggested?" Luxcius smiled and spoke.

"Tiamat, mother."

The Situation Worsens

The One then stopped and questioned the wisdom of Luxcius's choice. "Luxcius, Tiamat is young and a great deal more feminine. Don't you think it is wise to choose someone older, perhaps imbued with the male-like positive propulsive, the needed vitality to undergo something of this tumultuous challenge?"

Luxcius pleaded.

"No, your majesty. I believe Tiamat is the perfect choice. It is because of his feminine preponderance. The lost ones will need a nurturing environment in which to support their reclamation."

The One seemed to comprehend the thoughtfulness of Luxcius's plan and responded.

"All right, my son. Your plan has merit and seems well thought out. What will you call Tiamat, that we may know him by his new form?"

Luxcius paused before responding.

"Mother," he said smiling, "I thought why not use his true name, it is a good name. And he will be the footstool of your compassion and love."

The One looked at Luxcius and smiled.

"Very Well, my son, we give you, our blessing."

Luxcius's Plan

Luxcius was the One's Arch Chancellor and favored first son above all others of the unfallen. Luxcius would need special help for Tiamat's transformation. For this, he would choose a little-known group of immortals that were specialists with change and metamorphosis. These were the Varagonites. They existed in a remote region beyond the realm of the Djinn, called the Straights of Varagae. And specific to these most unusual creatures were the Seraphim.

Luxcius found the Varagonites in his exploration of the regions at the rim of the Djinn collective. The space in the Straights behaved very much like Praxxis. The energy was dense and more water-like and moved, changing direction, and swaying like an ocean's current. Luxcius found it difficult to navigate the water-like region without exercising control of his conscious center.

In his expansion, following the One's directive, he wanted to explore the interchange of love as other species experienced it. The Seraphim became interested in this fresh energy. It intrigued them with the quality of openness and trust, something that seemed contrary to their experience of the Djinn. That Luxcius emerged out of the Djinn represented a mystery to them.

Unlike most immortals existing in an androgynous state, having both male and female elements within the same being, the Varagonites could alter their male and female qualities at will. Though they remained with their unique male or female element, they were changelings. They also loved to alter their

Luxcius's Plan

age. At one moment, they could be old and, in the next moment, mere children.

Luxcius explained to the Varagonites the unique situation of his fallen brothers. He expressed his unusual request to integrate Tiamat one of Luxcius' closest friends, into a planet. Tiamat needed to exhibit all the qualities of density within the fallen's dream state universe yet remain in conscious harmony with the One's awareness.

Arajixx, Chief Magi Dragon of the Seraphim responded to Luxcius's request. Though Arajixx was mildly interested in Luxcius' problem, he seemed preoccupied and nonchalant.

"Hmmm." Arajixx murmured while he rubbed his furry chin. It's a most unusual request, but it's an interesting problem. Integrating this kind of being into something of an illusory object that also appears dead yet must remain conscious and flexible to the light of your Djinn is a challenge. We think it may be manageable."

Sensing the challenge for Arajixx Luxcius expressed concern.

"But you can do it…. right?" Arajixx's many eyes widened.

"Oh, my! Oh yes. We can do it. We love these sorts of challenges."

Luxcius exhaled with relief.

"Good!" Luxcius said. "Then we must proceed with the utmost urgency."

Arajixx smiled. "Our Magik is supreme amongst all those with the skill."

After an indeterminate period, Arajixx selected a large

illusory body lying in the 5th orbit around a small twin red sun system at the rim of a galactic spiral called Miramay. Tiamat completed his transformation and integration into the illusory planet. But this was just the first of many challenges that Luxcius faced. Within his plan for the fallen brothers, he needed to create a strong identified attachment, which would keep them focused on the new planet while he could implement his rehabilitation program. To accomplish this, Luxcius asked Arajixx to manifest polarized life forms on the surface of Tiamat. These would function as hosts to the fallen ones.

Arajixx could not comprehend this concept completely but complied. The importance of a strong lower life form, capable of providing the hosting attributes, required an evolutionary development. Arajixx considered many life forms from his home world as models. The various changeling forms might reflect unfolding lower spiritual levels, present within these fallen Stellar Minds.

With each of the five illusory planes of existence, down to the Astral Plane, five elements were magickly expressed as water, fire, Earth, and air. Then to complete the connection to the Djinn awareness, the lower spirit invoked was called the Akasha.

The creatures springing out of the sea on Tiamat emerged eventually upon the land and filled the atmosphere around Tiamat. the ecosystem was balanced. Arajixx believed the most desirable lower form of life would need to exist on the surface. Surface life would appear last, representing the strengths found in all developed species there.

It would be a long period before the sophistication of the land creatures appeared. The chief Magi believed only then could the chosen life form support and handle the immense force of the androgynous consciousness of the Stellar Minds. Arajixx discovered the radiation emerging from the larger of the two suns was far too intense and would endanger life forms on the surface. So, he created a canopy around the planet to mitigate that radiation. He uttered the Vril to magnetize further the planet to suspend the atmosphere and keep it attached to the surface.

Meanwhile, Luxcius created a staging area with the chief Magi Arajixx on the second planet from the glorious sun, which he named Vaness (Venus).

For the Tiamat to have a guiding principle for the planned rehabilitation, Arajixx created a porthole in the One passing through the glorious sun. The porthole would provide intelligent information from the higher worlds to flow through this system of planets that orbited around the porthole.

Another Stellar Mind, Sukon, assisted Luxcius in the rehabilitation process, managing the light-unifying program flowing through the porthole. The light from the light worlds carried the important balance needed for the unifying growth principle of all polarized life on the planets in the system. The light from the solar orb would also provide perfect temperatures for maximum possible evolutionary development. Sukon would supply the unifying principle of unconditional love unique to the One's realm. This porthole became known, in man's ancient history, as the Sun God.

Luxcius asked Arajixx to keep the 2nd planet Vaness in a gaseous state, as a place for the fallen Stellar Minds to remain suspended until Tiamat became ready for their infusion. Arajixx predetermined the only polarized life form which could sustain the force of the Stellar Mind consciousness would be a primate, a distant cousin of Arajixx' home world.

This kind of life form would be the pinnacle of evolutionary life on the planet. The primate would contain all genetic mutations from all of five elements, providing the best hope as a host species. Still, with all Arajixx' planning, there was no guarantee of a lower polarized life form merging with such a greater form of consciousness.

Arajixx was quick to suggest his plan was experimental.

"Luxcius, you must realize, we Magi have never done before. These diverse examples of lower biological forms of life would never come into contact, in such an intimate way."

Luxcius grunted with defiance.

"Don't you think I know this, little one? This situation is unique. It calls for radical solutions. I have complete confidence in your powers to achieve this unreasonable feat of magikal engineering."

Arajixx shrugged, not being accustomed to flattery.

"We wanted you to know the odds. Lower evolution by Magik is unpredictable and against what we normally do."

Luxcius rebutted.

"Consider the odds of the One emerging within the Djinn! He went on. Of course, It hasn't been done before! You

Luxcius's Plan

haven't done it yet!"

Arajixx returned with some humility.

"Yes, sire, we'll hope for the best."

They set the stage on Vaness and Luxcius's plan was well underway. The plan was clever in its essence. He hoped to provide a world where the fallen could relax in their illusion, then help them focus on reclaiming their consciousness. This would give Lucius the opportunity to help them organize their direction from the meandering energy. At the same time, Sukon, the solar logos, would superimpose a loving, guiding, unifying principle from the light worlds, encouraging them to remember their origins, and eventually allow their return to the whole of the One.

Meanwhile, in Tiamat, the early stages of violent development wound down to isolated volcanic action and severe tropical storms. Heavy rains developed into frequent monsoons and created a lush tropical jungle environment of flower and fauna. The rain forests were thick with popul and banyan trees, giant ferns, and undergrowth. Jungles thrived on the rich volcanic soils and teamed with insects and small animals scurrying about, seeking for food while building shelters from the elements.

A sea surrounded the new world, polarized with one great landmass on most of the surface. I would know later this great continent as Gwandana.

In a small eastern coastal area of the continent, the first primates appeared. They were small creatures living in the banyan trees. These early primates were very agile, with their six fingered hands and feet, three long and three shorter and with a long tenacious tail. The tail, often used to hang upside down, left their hands and feet free to grab fruit dangling from other trees and clinging vines nearby. Their large round eyes, developed to see within the mantel of vapor covering most of the landmass, gave them a striking appearance.

The thick mantel changed the light, giving a pale quality of semi-darkness. Arajixx expected much from the mantel. It was key and provided a gentle shield from the harsh heat and light for all the young and tender species still under development. Later, this mantel would eventually break. These early primates were the great ancestors of the modern-day Lemurs. This area of the continent became known as Lemuria, the land of the lemurs.

The unsuspecting lemurs hung carefree in the comfort of their domiciles above the ground while far above and beyond them, on Vaness, other androgynous lifeforms poised to descend upon them.

The lemurs looked up one day to see bright lights. Like meteors crashing through the dense vapor of the mantel in blinding flashes raining onto the surface. This intrusion disturbed the lemurs. Often, they saw these showers of light before, from real meteorites streaming into the Tiamat's atmosphere. Looking on below, the lights did not hit the surface as before. Scampering around within the high trees, they looked on with great curiosity at their would-be hosts.

The Stellar Minds rushed to the unsuspecting primates attaching themselves. The lemurs cried in pain, falling from

Luxcius's Plan

the tree's dead to the ground below. One after the other, each fell dead. It was clear to Arajixx, as he expected, the first infusion failed, showing the primate's unsuitability for the infusion. The first root race of Tiamat failed, now a group of lifeless heaps on the rainforest floor.

Luxcius rushed in with great expectations. He found his brothers dazed and confused and without living hosts. The Stellar Minds looked upon him with a sense of bewilderment.

"Why can we not find cause to meld with these creatures?"

Luxcius responded with compassion.

"Patience my brothers, we will bring this to fruition soon."

Meanwhile, Luxcius approached the chief Magi Arajixx with concern.

"Why are my brothers without hosts Arajixx?"

Arajixx answered.

"Noble prince, you must understand this is a work of greater difficulty. We must adjust the primate's nervous system to adapt to the shock of greater consciousness. Remember, these creatures have never been self-aware! Perhaps it will be better after the next change."

Luxcius now replied calmly.

"I'm counting on you Arajixx. You must succeed with this. My plan depends upon your success!"

Arajixx replied. "By you lead, Sire."

Arajixx continued making genetic adjustments with his magikal skill to raise the frequency of the primate's nervous system to another level of sophistication. Once again, the Stellar Minds descended on the changed creatures. But once again, as they attached, the Lemurs cried out in pain, even though the attachment sustained the Stellar Minds a little longer. Still, more lay dead on the forest floor. The seed of the second root race failed.

Arajixx looked on with concern. With Luxcius peering over him, he remained steadfast with his mission to succeed. Once again, he changed the primate's genetic frequency, lifting their nervous systems to yet another level of sophistication.

This time, the fallen Stellar Minds descended upon the primates, and their cry sounded different. It was not pain they expressed, but surprise. The third seeding was a glorious success. They lived, and further, they became a marriage of animal and spirit of a higher order. Soon, they descended from their tree domiciles. Other primates, untouched, looked on below with greater curiosity. The new primates behaved differently compared to their counterparts. Under the greater influence of their spiritual symbionts, climbed down to the ground foraging on the surface. Thus, the third root race of man in Lemuria had begun.

Best Laid Plans

Beliel soon learned of Luxcius's plan to recover the lost Stellar Minds. He knew Luxcius exhibited a certain similarity to the Djinn in his ambition. For Luxcius, it was a weakness. For the One Luxcius's innate quality of ambition would become the One weakness.

Still disgruntled with Bael's decision about the One Beliel believed this might be the opportunity he hoped for. If he could use this ambition of Luxcius to detour the One's progress, he could assert Bael had made a poor decision to let the One live. He could use this to undermine the Council's confidence of Bael. Then he would improve his chances of dislodging Bael from the Supreme Council seat and thus rise to become Supreme Chancellor of the Council himself.

This represented another contrasting point between the world of the Djinn and the realm of the One. Hierarchy can lead to competition among the ranks through ambition. Without hierarchy in the One's realm, ambition is non-existent. So, there could be no competition without the driving force of ambition. One's will of is also common to all, so ambition could not arise, at least in principle. The One would not expect the effect of Luxcius's ambition until much later. A complete dedication to unconditional love and compassion would not allow the One to view the faults and limitations or their effects. The One is innocent of these things. She does not vibrate in these ways. Beliel's plan to undermine Luxcius was about to unfold. The One didn't see it coming.

All seemed to be well underway on Tiamat as the Stellar

Minds continued to influence the primates, altering their behavior. They ceased climbing trees and continued to forage on the ground for food. Now they sought caves for shelter, huddling together for warmth and mutual protection.

The fallen became engrossed with the basic elements of Tiamat along with the pleasure of knuckle walking on the surface. It was exhilarating to feel the warm, soft soil of Tiamat receiving their feet and hands while they explored the joy of traversing the surface. Others explored the other elements as well, like the new experience of playing in the water. Though after several drownings, it didn't take long to figure out the nostrils were not suited for plunging below the surface without incurring breathing difficulty.

The Magi continued to assist in the alteration of the primates, facilitating a smooth continued symbiont relationship. They sped up the loss of hair, facilitating ease of movement in the water. A new bridge covering the nostrils allowed a greater measure of protection from the unexpected water entering the lungs. The land walkers rose to an erect posture while both species lost the need for tails since their complete abandonment of the trees.

The primates needed less physical development since the water environment supported the weight of their bodies. Water primates remained small in stature, while they focused more on mental pursuits. The vast and continuous mental focus caused their craniums to swell from the added convolutions of extra growth. Meanwhile, the land walkers developed powerful bodies, with very muscular limbs and a taller stature by comparison.

The Magi were confident of the early stages of primate development and showed good evolutionary choices on their part. Confident the primates were strong enough to withstand the intense energy of the large red sun, Arajixx ordered the thick mantel surrounding Tiamat to be lifted. Now, in the bright light of the solar orb, Sukon forced further changes for both species.

The water primates changed their skin to reflect a salamander-like quality able to sustain a constant exposure of bright light and water made a distinct greenish-yellow pigment in their smooth skin. Whereas the land walkers became thick skinned, having more of a leather-like texture, with a ruddy-red coloration in their pigment. The land walkers also kept patches of fur on their bodies to protect more delicate areas such as the chest, groin, and back. The top of the head and face were furry to protect from the strong rays of Sukon.

Not all Stellar Minds gave way to Luxcius's plan for a return to the One's realm. One such Stellar Mind expressed strong resentment to the symbiosis of Stellar consciousness with these conjured hairy beasts. His name was Pan. Pan took the option of the whole idea in fact but conceded the need for a greater focus of their energy. So, he put forth his own claims. Approaching Luxcius, he complained.

"Brother Luxcius, why should I, or anyone else, accept this way of expression? I have sufficient imaginary powers to develop my form to express. We do not need this bestial form. It seems limited. It repulses and does not suit my desire."

Luxcius defended Arajixx's efforts.

"Bother Pan, do you not see the importance of this place, Tiamat, and these unique forms of life chosen by the Magi of Seraphim? You would do well to choose these, as they proved to be the most functional in this environment."

Pan continued to protest.

"Lucifer, we can appreciate your efforts, but we are not the only ones to dispute these lower forms and their limitations. I see the value of this place for us, but we wish to apply our own forms in which to express here. We will not stay here. We will go to another part of this world and find our own way."

With that declaration, Pan left, despite Lucifer's protests, along with several others, to an area further south on the continent. I knew later this area as the Galapagos Islands.

Pan and his followers defiance upset Lucifer, but his troubles were just beginning. Beliel had descended into this earthly sphere to sow the seeds of dissent among those that lived as symbionts within the primates.

Beliel set to work behind Luxcius's back, pointing out to the fallen. There was a most curious energy, called spirit, providing the life of the primates. It was the primary source for the procreative agent responsible for their propagation as a physical species. Beliel appealed to the fallen, to notice this sexual force flowing between the primates during their mating.

Beliel suggested further, if they were to engage in this mating process, they could understand the unifying principle of spirit. They could have greater knowledge at the most fundamental levels of being. Then, to capture his seduction, he promised them a fast return to the unified state, and an end to their suffering!

The Stellar Minds took Beliel's suggestion to heart. Beliel left them to ponder this and returned to the realm of the Djinn, knowing he had planted the seeds of discontent. He knew it would only be a matter of time before they all are lost. Beliel's evil seed already took root. It puzzled them. How could they reach a close quarter embracing of this act, when they are by nature androgynous? How could they feel the unity of this polarity, of this joining, unless it polarized them themselves?

Many approached Luxcius with troubled minds and many questions. They petitioned Luxcius to separate them from their androgynous state, into male and female aspects. Explaining that they, not Beliel, had discovered this procreative energy called spirit. The Stellar Minds wanted to experience this sexual force exchanged between the primates during their mating process. Arguing, in this way, they could understand better the unifying principle.

The Stellar Minds were convincing. Their arguments played on Luxcius's weakness of ambition. Luxcius was desperate for his plan to succeed. Anything that would decrease the chances of his plan to fail, he favored. So, he agreed to give them what they wanted. With the help of the Magi. The Magi separated all into separate male and female aspects of each Stellar Mind.

Excited in their anticipation of experiencing their newfound perspectives, they rejoined the primates, looking forward to a quick end to their suffering. They merged with each of their gender, male to male and female to female. Luxcius looked on with some trepidation. He wondered now what the outcome would be? He knew this had to be a mistake, but he hoped for the best.

Soon after many generations, Luxcius's worst fears realized, the Stellar Minds disintegrated through the offspring. In the first mating, the Stellar consciousness fractured into halves, then with the next generation, they disintegrated again into quarter levels and so on, until there was none sufficient to remember even being splintered at all. It was too late. All the Stellar Minds became lost in complete and utter chaos, with no way of retrieving them. Luxcius, frantic about what to do, lamented.

"What shall I tell the One? How can I explain away this disaster?"

He paced back and forth, racking his burdened mind for an answer to this dilemma. Alas, he had no answer…they're lost to oblivion, and that was the end. His plan, now in shambles, his pride and arrogance, was to be his undoing. There would be no saving grace for him, for he had destroyed his brothers out of his love for them. But he could not see the terrible ambition behind his motive…in this, he was blind.

He turned to Arajixx for help.

"Dear Arajixx, is there nothing you can do?" Arajixx shrugged his shoulders with a sigh.

"Dear prince, I'm sorry for you. Taking your brothers apart was easy. We have no way to find them, to put them back together. For in the mating process of the primates, they descended through the offspring randomly. The precise pathway is unknown. They don't remember who they are, so we can't ask them to stand up and identify themselves."

Arajixx turned as he was leaving, his voice trailing off.

"It's a terrible thing, but there is nothing we can do for you. We are sympathetic to your loss. We bid you condolences and farewell, for there is nothing we can do here anymore." Luxcius nodded, first in the affirmative, then shook his head from side to side in despair.

Pan and his followers arrived in the Galapagos. They wasted no time to explore their creations of their own combinations of animal-man-like creatures. There was half primate with half horses, half primates, and half birds, even half primate combinations of fish, which Pan called mermen and mermaids. It was endless. Soon they grew tiresome of this fruitless escapade. They knelt to ask the One's forgiveness.

The One appeared before them, full of compassion in their plight.

"Do not fear, my children, rejoice instead! You have seen the finality of this sorrowful path you all have taken. Can you not see, in our continence, the unconditional love we have for you? Return to the inner fold at once. All that is ours is yours to partake."

Pan responded face down, prostrated before the One. "Mother of us all, please know we love you and wish to respect your wishes, but we decline. With your consent, may we request to remain here, in this world, to continue with this work? It is your love and devotion that is projected. We wish to remain in the Astral realm of this illusory world, where we can best maintain all the living things here, to assist Tiamat in his expression on your behalf, since the chief Magi Arajixx of the Saraphim is no longer here to guide this manifestation."

The One smiled at Pan. Then She expressed a great wave of blue and gold light, full of love and compassion for him and all his followers, which she showered upon them.

"Blessed are all my children and their good works. It is in this way that our realm of freedom shall flourish and propagate throughout all the lower kingdoms. So, let it be said, so let it be done. May tidings of great joy flow in your beingness and provide continued help to your brothers, who are still struggling to embrace their depleted condition on Tiamat. All your efforts shall offer greater possibilities, so they may remember that our love offers the divine beauty and grace of continued life as it bounds on Tiamat. Now where is my son Luxcius? And where are the rest of my children?"

The Defiance

Luxcius took refuge in one of Tiamat's higher mountains, near the center of the continent. The altitude gave him some elevated solace while he tried to recover his composure from the irreversible effects of his misdeeds. Beliel seized upon this raw moment for young Luxcius, with an opportunity to council him.

Beliel approached Luxcius, appearing behind him.

"It never ceases to amaze me how this young one can just run rough-shod over all her mistakes and not taking responsibility for any of them. Don't you agree, young prince?"

Luxcius was startled for a moment and turned, thinking he was alone. He lowered his head before answering.

"I don't know. I don't understand how this calamity could have happened."

Beliel continued to cajole Luxcius.

"Luxcius, it was a good plan. You only tried to help. You're not accountable for trying to keep the fallen ones happy and satisfied. It's not your fault. They are the ones who asked for the separation…yes? The One should praise you. Instead, she is making you responsible for her lack of foresight."

"Luxcius, it would not surprise me that the One will go even further!"

Luxcius looked up at Beliel. His eyes widened as he asked.

"What do you mean, further?"

Beliel could not contain his pleasure. He turned a smile at his reaction. He continued twisting his cruel knife deeper into Luxcius's heart.

"Why do you think she would keep you here, in this forsaken illusory?"

"Are you not watching over her abomination? The One is ashamed of what She has created. She needed someone to monitor, to cover up her disaster. So, it doesn't become an embarrassment for her with the collective. Frankly Luxcius I think it shows a lack of respect for you and your abilities and more…it's below your stature!"

Luxcius stood up from the rock he crouched on. His eyes were now red with fury. Luxcius paced back and forth for a few moments, struggling with his thoughts, trying to grasp Beliel's accusations. He did not want to accept the torment he felt from the truth of his part in this debacle. The awful pain of what he had done was hard to bear. He drank in Beliel's words, quenching his thirst for an escape from the pain.

He stood now with his back to Beliel, mumbling to himself.

"How could she do this? I've done nothing wrong! I was the only one to come forth, to help the One out of this dilemma… the only one!"

His thinking became a mirror, fertile ground for Beliel's poisonous seeds. He could not see one more clever or more sinister and more ancient in the ways of deceit duping him.

Encouraged by Beliel Luxcius convinced himself he was without blame on the whole matter. He believed his intentions were honorable, well meant. Then, he turned his suffering mind to self-deceit and diversion. He filled his heart with hurt, replacing the shame he felt before. How could the One dare to accuse him? Beliel, now convinced Luxcius, is prepared for the One's arrival. The evil he caused now firmly set into motion. All he had to do now was watch his evil plot unfold. Pleased with himself, Beliel felt assured that the Supreme Council seat was all but his for the taking.

The Defiance

Not long after, The One arrived on Tiamat and called out to Luxcius.

"Luxcius. Come forth to us and give us your plan's progress for my children."

Luxcius appeared before the One, thinking he would stand ready to defend his actions, but he prostrated himself before the shining continence of the One.

"I am here, mother. He said in a low and trembling voice."

The One looked down upon her most cherished of all children with wonder.

"Luxcius, she inquired. Why do you cower before me, trembling? I want to see my children. Where are they? We cannot feel them now!"

Luxcius continued in a low voice.

"Yes mother. I have something terrible to report. Your children ..my brothers, are all dead to you now, for all eternity. And it is my fault! In my arrogance and pride to build up myself for your sake, I have set them apart, polarized their androgyny. They have entered an unholy state. I lost them in the offspring of the animals they inhabited."

"How is this possible, my son? How have you divided them?" The One bade.

Luxcius continued.

"I have broken their eternal bond into male and female mother, so they could experience this lower form of procreative current of spirit, an artifact of bi-polar life here."

The One was silent. She turned her back on Luxcius to grasp the severity of this crime. She turned back again, with tempered anger in her voice. It thundered beyond the four corners of the compass as she bellowed.

"This unholy act is not for my sake! It is for yours! What were you thinking? We are shocked at your lack of love, understanding, and compassion. We struggle to believe you would allow such an abomination to occur. Luxcius, your heart is clouded… with ambition… with lust. My most cherished of sons have wounded my heart. You have betrayed my trust in you! You have brought shame and sadness into our fold. What have you to say for yourself?"

Luxcius did not respond as he noticed the One now shaken. Not until now did he feel this terrible feeling brought on by his misdeed. He could bear the terrible sense. The One's innocence of love and joy had shattered. It was as if he had put a thumb into the eye of the One, so she could not see beauty, love and joy any more… only the pain.

The One wept for the first time since her awakening. Luxcius wept also, for the terrible woe he brought to his mother. Shame draped over him like a great dark shroud. He dropped all thoughts of his defiance. For those moments, he shared the burden of pain together with his mother.

The One began.

"Luxcius, the grave nature of this act, brings heaviness to our heart. This leads us to consider the need to find a resolution to this problem. We will create a way for our children to find their way out of this chaos. This will not be easy. We have taken the way of love and harmony from them. They have much responsibility for this. It is not sufficient for them to be restored. We cannot just let this pass. You and they must atone for this great sin against the whole of us."

"The solution must also contain the atonement. I hold you responsible as well. You must also atone for this transgression.

So, it is our will that you remain here in Tiamat, along with all of those who assisted in this calamity."

"I want you to comprehend the seriousness of this act. You will accomplish this by overseeing their rehabilitation and ultimate reconstitution until they are whole again. Your pain will be great, but it will be a healing pain. You will contemplate your actions here, on Tiamat by being in their presence, suffering with them, in their separation. This will burn into your heart, for all time, the importance of the unity of all."

Luxcius could not believe his senses. What Beliel said passed. The tears of sorrow turned to anger.

The One continued.

"We used the results of your plan for those lost to their greater good and understanding. From now on, they will know all the fruits of their separation. In the polarity of light and dark, their innocence lost. They shall know all there is without grace, but with greater effort. They will struggle to climb their way out of the chaos by their slow and deliberate reconstruction."

"They will not have love but learn to develop their love and respect for all life through the lower order of life they have chosen. They will work to bring divine essence to rise within the loins of the base and unholy bodies they cherish."

"Henceforth, it shall be by my love and memory of those that have fallen. They will come to remember themselves through the discovery of what was lost. They will return and return until they find they have lost all that in this world of illusion. Then and only then will they rejoin their stellar halves and be whole again… to ascend to the love and light of unity and neutrality as fully rehabilitated members of our family."

"It will be from their choice that they no longer know us. They will come to know death and birth and through it they will know what is good and holy by the sweat of their brow. Then they will count the hours of their passing and lament and then shall they know the value. It will develop and build to sustain the vibrations. By their efforts, they shall realize the glory that is unity with the whole. So let it be said, so let it be done."

Luxcius could hear no more. He could not contain the anger any longer. His jaw tightened as he exploded with fury.

"All I tried to do was help this unfortunate situation by creating a way for the fallen to return under divine supervision. You were aware of what I was planning. It was going well until this incident. Now, you want to make me and those who helped me responsible."

"I think you are being harsh in your judgment on this matter. I don't deserve this maltreatment and mistrust. I believe you are afraid of the embarrassment, and you want to cover up your part in this by making me the scapegoat."

"You want me to remain here…fine! You want me to assist the fallen to return to your fold by overseeing the continued process of their birth cycling? Well, I have a different idea! I'll tell you what I think."

"I will assist them, but not to return to you. I will make it our concern to make sure they understand the true nature of your love and compassion. We will show them a different way. We will show them my way. I will teach them about the cruelty of your love and the dissatisfaction that comes from an allegiance to you and your ways. I will become your worst nightmare, Mother. I will remain here, yes. But I will make sure that your lost children never return and never come out of chaos. I will make it my sole achievement to undermine every brother trying to rise from oblivion. I will do all that is in my power to make sure they will not achieve the greater light. And I will deceive them and will bring brother against brother, so this situation in Tiamat will become your greatest example of failure for all to see."

The One, stunned by Luxcius's defiance, responded.

"Well, my son, it saddens me to hear you say this, but I will not stop you in this. To do so would mean the will to express freely would come to a halt. But I cannot abide with you to teach your style of sedition against the whole while you still live within the whole. This would be an abomination in a holy place. So, by your declaration of separation, we banish you from our realm until the day comes. You will recant your defiance of love, justice and compassion for all that is righteous."

"This world, Tiamat, shall be a place of light and dark. Our will for greater freedom in this place shall remain. All will have an equal opportunity to seek the light on their own, by their own effort. So be it they do it under your terrible curse."

Beliel watched them from afar. He could not help but feel a certain delight.

He laughed and thought to himself,

"How easy it is to deceive the young one. Perhaps this will be easier than I thought."

The Struggle Begins

The situation worsened with the fallen. Luxcius's threats to block further development and recovery of the lost did not discourage the One. She would restore them to their rightful place in her realm with whatever it required or how long it might take. There were many issues for her to consider.

Whatever steps she might take would involve the rift between the light worlds of timeless eternity and the immobile state of the fallen in time. Time, an additional issue rising out of the fallen consciousness of their dream state, would hamper any direct approach to the problem.

First, she established some indirect contact with them by creating a link from their dream state to the genetic code already established within each animal's body. In the animal structure, there would be a consistent genetic string of potential growth maintained through each offspring. Through each string, the One could attach a minor aspect or quality of the fallen consciousness. Then synchronize it with the experiences of the animal's life. In this way, she created a traceable sequence of life experience.

She could embed spiritual concepts and feelings into each aspect of the fallen consciousness. These could relate to each daily experience of the animal. This might lead the animal host to disturb the fallen that is dreaming. This might motivate the fallen ones to awaken. Then if the fallen could awaken, it would feel the pain of the longing. If enough of that awakening pain occurs, it might probe the pain to find and reveal something of what is missing in its life. There was only

The Struggle Begins

one catch with this approach. The One wasn't sure that there was enough left within the animal through the procreative line to grasp anything recognizable.

So, the agony of something missing would have to be very strong, present, and pressing to irritate the life of the animal and the remnant consciousness. On the surface, this might seem cruel but later perhaps, interpreted as harsh. The One decided to take that risk for the sake of the fallen. The One knew this could prove maddening to the remnant consciousness of the Stellar Mind. She paused many times to consider how terrible it was! Seeking a resolution in this way and forcing the experience of pain and suffering could drive the fallen further away from her.

The fallen androgynous nature now divided into male and female polarized aspects reduced with each offspring and posed additional challenges for the One. A consistent and integrated path of experience could accumulate and provide pointers to failures and successes. But something complicated it. Each experience needed to address both the male and female perspectives. With the connection to the whole of the One broken, there could be no immediate success in reaching the exalted state. She knew only in the exalted state of being could they reach the memory of their essence.

Then the One experienced a divine epiphany. She realized that with luxcius there to dissuade the fallen; they needed another example alongside the fallen to model the right actions and awareness. Thus, her plan to extend herself and her way not only in the quantum field of the Djinn but to extend her way into the lower kingdoms created in the fall.

She would create a new being not unlike herself, yet these new creatures could sustain the middle and lower existence vibrations, which was something she could not do for long. It would make these new beings out of the middle Kingdom within but carry the sheath of the lower kingdom vibration. They would represent her emissaries. They would be avatars living on Tiamat to assist the fallen and establish her way on the planet.

So, the One extended through the grace of her witness aspect, an embodiment of the essence of herself. This would be the divine pattern of unity as an imprint, a reflection of the light world consciousness. These would be changelings of a mixed order of lower vibrations and middle vibrations with the over-vibration of light. She would call them Nome-Lu-Lu. They would come to live in a paradise setting in a lush, tropical zone of the planet, near its equator.

Meanwhile, the One needed to channel the automatic genetic unfolding of each animal. The animal bodies would change to reflect the shape of the experience mixed with the shape of the animal consciousness. Now, with this new continuous adaptation, the animal's body would not unfold without the overriding factor of the influence on its shape.

In modern man's concepts of spirituality, we believe someone pours a 'soul' into the body at birth or at some moment thereafter. It would seem, however, that this is not the case. In the nine-month gestation process of the birthing cycle, the

The Struggle Begins

body forms because of the metamorphosis of the spiritual force shaping the essence of the animal. From that moment on, the animal would be a true symbiotic shape of animal instincts and the genetic breeding of all prior species and the imbuing of the life force of the One's memory.

All of this had to happen quickly. The One was battling the rapid loss and fragmentation of the fallen with successive generations. They fractured at a speed which was exponential.

Each rebirth exacerbated the problem, as the shock and transition in each death and birth cycle would erase the memory of what was before. What they gained in the previous experience, they could lose to the new offspring.

The One needed to capture and keep their experiences. Then, the stored experiences could bolster the new experience of the next offspring later. The One would use the Law of Resonance to define the absolute connectedness of all things by resonant rapport. She meant to reintegrate the experiences into another fragment of the remnant. If something is like another thing, they attract it to the first thing because of its similarity. We know it as 'like attracts like.'

The One accomplished this by changing the quality of the outermost surface of Tiamat's higher spiritual level, called the Akasha. The Astral level of Tiamat is the life-bearing barrier containing the planet's life force. The One made this barrier a little sticky, like a spider's web. It would then catch the thoughts and feelings of all sentient life passing through it. Upon the death transition, it would pick up previous experiences representing markers while returning through the birthing transition.

The barrier was intelligent, with a sticky quality. Unique to each remnant, then governed by the experiences of each driven by their genetic code. It would function as a personal tracker relating to that remnant's experience. It would tag the experiences stored. Those experiences would be available to future offspring with a similar genetic structure.

Expecting the potential growth of each remnant, the brilliance of the One allowed for a mutual sharing of other's experiences as they gathered more consciousness. In time, this would encourage remembrance of the essence of the Stellar Mind and the remembrance of the One.

Still, there was the overriding influence that Luxcius might play on all of this. The One suspected that Luxcius meant to do what he set out to do, that is confused, disorient and dishevel whatever positive encouragement which might arise.

The One also did not expect that while the remnant consciousness lay sleeping and dreamed of itself, it would develop worlds upon worlds of other consciousness as ideas and concepts, including layers of philosophy, myths, and legends. These sprung forth from their buried memories regarding the true nature of 'the living non-physical light worlds' This would later become the groundswell of difficulty that proved to be the most trying in all her challenges. She wanted to recapture the imagination of her lost children. Two very important issues stood in the way of that desire.

The chief Magi Arajixx reformed her son Tiamat and magically infused him to this physical planet in the fifth orbit around the red sun Sukon. Luxcius was on to her plan. He countered by choosing to use the fragile elements of dreams and thought form patterns existing within the animal matrix to infuse his greatest disabling gift to his brothers, and that was the element of doubt!

Meanwhile, another wrinkle appeared, catching both the One and Luxcious off guard. The solar orb, Sukon was not the only sun of this system. Sukon inhabited the larger of two suns, known as Sol. But there was another twin dwarf star incomplete and not giving of greater light. That dwarf star also carried along with it 7 planetary bodies. Its orbit was much larger and more elliptical. Its path was long and more obscured by the remnants of the solar system's emergence known today as the Orc Cloud. It is a place of cosmic dust, asteroid debris, and ice crystals.

Eventually the dwarf star, with its 7 orbiting bodies, returned to enter the perihelion, the closest arc of the elliptical path around Sol and brought with it a much larger planet in direct collision with Tiamat. The Nome-lu-lu sensed the danger and descended into deep caverns below the surface. On impact, it destroyed much of Tiamat, leaving a ring of asteroids in the belt between Mithra (known today as Mars) and Ganymede (known today as Jupiter). The largest piece of Tiamat swung away and rotated out of its 5th orbit and reentered into the third orbit between Vaness (now called Venus) and Mithra (Mars) Almost all perished in the impact except those that were underground within the large remnant survived. Only Eight Nome-Lu-Lu survived along with some animals.

The One approached Arajixx to apply his skill to help mend the lower planetary entity still containing Tiamat's energy field. Arajixx brought the remnant into balance by adding the water element while sustaining the spin of the remnant into balance on its own axis. The dwarf star returned to its outer most aphelion arc with the rest of its orbiting planets. The One named the dwarf star Nemeses.

The One told the surviving eight Nome-Lu-Lu to remain within the deep recesses of the remnant until conditions on the surface regained a modicum of normalcy. Arajixx felt Tiamat had been altered and should assume a new identity. She agreed. Arajixx called the remnant Earth.

Today believers feel God made all the beauty on the Earth. This makes sense at first. Someone would think that the One in her love for the fallen would want to surround her children with such beauty. This is not the case. It was by original design from Arajixx that made the Earth attractive and like Tiamat. He felt it would be a good idea to make familiar and attractive surroundings for the wayward and wondering fallen. Then why would the One want to add to the illusion here? This would be at cross-purposes for her. This would make it even more difficult to break free of the illusion. With the physical world being so beautiful. No one would ever want to leave! The One was so devastated by the unforeseen calamity she could no longer stay in the lower vibratory state and returned to the light worlds in her lament.

This brings up the point that attachments here for the world and all the things in it including loved ones, created a binding

The Struggle Begins

energy that distracted the fallen. The experiences as imprints would never find a genuine sense of themselves and their origins. The single most important aspect of this layering in the dream state is the insistence that the physical world is the only living reality. This fundamental belief blocks any possibility of awakening to the truth of the illusion. The dreams that the fallen were dreaming seemed real then and through their children are as real today. What was unseen would fall into the category of childish imagination? We all can remember the painful day of growing up. Then 'Imaginary things' get eliminated as our adult life begins.

This proves later to be unfortunate, leaving the adult the one most capable of making sense of all that is without child-like suppleness, now replaced with a goat-like disbelief in the unseen. The openness of the mind, like a child, is necessary for success. Luxcius saw this as his chance to close the book on the fallen.

Then the final straw which could undermine the fallen comes from Luxcius himself. First, the greatest lie ever told in myth and legend is that he doesn't exist or that the One doesn't exist either! But to furrow the brow further, he caused his new and insidious devourer of the hope of return to enter the Earth plane. He had introduced doubt to destroy the faith into the world.

This is his sublime and darkest contribution to the already overtaxed fallen mind. Just when one of the fallen imprints stands in the light, Luxcius drops that quiet little grenade into the back door of the unsuspecting mind. It becomes an almost certain silent killer of all faiths. Doubt in oneself and in life, in the One, brings down the mighty, the just, and the righteous from the highest exalted places. Much like a stone falling out of the sky.

[note to the reader:] Biblical scholars know for certain the doctrine of reincarnation was a part of the early biblical scriptures but removed later from the list of accepted canons along with obscure gospels declared heretical in the ecumenical council of the 4th century AD by the emperor Constantine.

The reason is common ignorance. Such knowledge requires self-responsibility, which is in short supply. If misused or misunderstood could detour or delay their spiritual development. Perhaps the ignorant men would feel unmotivated to change. Recurring lives eliminate timely improvement in their state of being and therefore might elicit them to procrastinate in their opportunities to develop.

If one were to scrutinize modern biblical scripture, they might find certain remarks within the accepted canons that refer to the doctrine of reincarnation indirectly.

For those who might accept this doctrine as a real possibility, the doctrine of transmigration often comes into the picture. That doctrine is about migrating from animals into human beings and back again through the process of retribution. This idea comes out of some Eastern-Indian cultures. The author believes these ideas to be a mixture of distortions handed down through many generations.

The doctrine of the 'soul' comes as distortions in the handing down of knowledge more often by word of mouth than in the written form. Many were illiterate at the time of its learning. The innate importance of previous experiences can serve as a reminder of the fallen of their origins and take on a significant importance for itself. It begins with the original idea of the One's desire to preserve what is lost. In time, then reduces to the idea the soul needs saving. This idea is fundamental to most religious sects today and with all Christendom.

The fundamental principle of the imprint is to awaken the remnant of the fallen Stellar Mind within everyone being. After this might occur will dissolve after each life sojourn on earth. They would refer to this as the 'crossing over.' There is no necessity to keep the individual personality of the ego self.

This idea does not sit well for most people. The common desire is to meet their maker in heaven after their death. They often interpret the concept of dissolving to mean annihilation. That said, it is important to realize the real purpose of the imprints is to remain stored intact in the Akasha as a record of the living being that lived life before. The expression remains living in this state as a living reference of all those experiences. They reference them as markers when the next imprint comes through with its agenda.

This is how the One created a consistent and accumulating experience within the family of experiences or bloodline of each of the fallen. Each imprint would represent an aspect of remembering through its discoveries in life or not. Hence the need to express imprints more than once.

The One still needed to deal with the difficulty in the

element of time. The time differential between the time-oriented Earth dream and the non-time eternal of heaven could create a synchronized set of experiences, with the non-synchronous emergence of an imprint.

The imprint might not arrive at the right time on Earth, leading to a life on earth lived without consequence, which happens sometimes. It means that a being could go through life being unfulfilled even though in the scheme of things; it is not important. Time is an illusion. So, how many lives it might take to accomplish the discovery is irrelevant to the One.

So, all imprints survive death as living records in the Akasha. These living records are complete and are interactive, meaning, if one were to go into the Akasha to meet and speak with Abraham Lincoln, he would respond spontaneously. He would be in the Akasha as he was in life, unaware he was anything other than a living president dealing with the issues of his time. You could talk with him and relate to him as you could with any living person.

A clarifying point in the One's system of reincarnation surrounds the common belief with many present-day people. One experiences many lives throughout time. One returns to live each life as a new personality, forgetting the previous personalities. This is true in the main. Each will, upon crossing over, lose its animating personality quality, but it will leave behind the record of its expression in life in the Akasha.

When an individual awakens, some memories of other life expressions will emerge in the life of the present consciousness. Its memory of other experiences will seem as real for the consciousness in the present. Those other life experiences will share those lives as its own. This sharing means that the individual may be closer to the gathering of itself into its higher consciousness.

Then the only remaining need is for it to meet its complement, its other half or twin. This twinning of consciousness happens at the close of an epoch when time is compressing.

Hundreds of thousands of years passed on the Earth. The primates continued to develop in their areas according to their environment. The water primates further refined their bodies through ongoing changes through each generation. Following the predilection of their mental behavior, their thoughts and ideas became the predominate focus of their existence. Their brain continued to grow disproportionate to the rest of their body and their cranium enlarged to adapt to their brain growth. Their body remained frail. The buoyancy of the liquid surrounding them compensated for the normal gravity on land.

The land walkers continued to grow tougher and more weathered to accommodate exposure to greater changes in temperature and the rugged terrain. Their need to defend themselves against other predators made them clever and aware of their surroundings. Their senses grew strong especially their sense of smell. For example, it was not uncommon that they could smell someone or some other creature many miles away be it friend or foe.

Their existence defined a continued effort to forage for food while trying to find better shelter from predators and the elements. Changing conditions in the harsh climate and the migrating food sources forced them to seek other locations to improve their situation. By necessity these primates became nomadic. Many explored lands further and further away from their origins as they followed the migrations of other beasts.

They migrated from regions of the great tropical East to the West over what would later be the Siberian tundra. They crossed the Bering Strait into the northern Alaskan wilderness and further west. Then they descended into yet another new land.

This land was strange and apparently uninhabited. They seemed psychically drawn to this new land right away. Active volcanoes and assorted flying creatures as well as smaller non-threatening beasts populated it. Most importantly, it seemed devoid of the dreaded Trok. The Trok (Tyrannosaurus-Rex or Thunder Lizard) was their most feared predator. It was a giant lizard that stood on its hind legs and powerful tail and then used its smaller front arms and claws and powerful jaws to grapple. Many have fought this beast, and many have not lived to tell the tale. It was a ferocious flesh eater.

They would settle in this land. Their new home later called Atlan and then finally becoming Atlantis. Later, the major continent broke into small continental masses and drifted apart because of volcanic, earthquake tectonic activity.

The nomads found themselves cutoff from their original homeland by water on all sides. The two species that dominated the continent continued to develop into different societies, one to the west and one to the east, as the Atlantean and Lemurian, respectively.

In time, the Atlanteans assimilated higher systems of organization from the small tribal groupings to more sophisticated clans and then into regional communities segregated according to specific skill sets. The Atlanteans organized the Atlantean regions into separate territories. They became complete societies unto themselves and ruled by overseers or governors of these minor kingdoms. They also carried their own standards or colors. The entire collection of territories would meet on special notable occasions. Later, a joint council of overseer/governors formed a ruling class over the entire continent as allied kings, representing the interests of their regional constituents. This became one of the first forms of centralized government in this society.

The Lemurian society did not organize into regions but remained as one collective group tied together by telepathic rapport. This rudimentary form of telepathic communication kept the Lemurians from developing a verbal language. Though they were non-verbal, they would later learn to speak some Atlantean language by necessity, because of trade and truce negotiations.

The staging area of Earth was a thorn in Luxcius' side and became an important issue to Beliel. He took a great deal of interest in this colony of Terran called the Lemurians. But the successful rehabilitation of the fallen would be a major stumbling block for Belial's plan to seize the Supreme Chancellor's seat of the Djinn High Council. Feeling the imperative that this experiment on the Earth had to fail would give him a chance to berate Bael's judgment later.

Beliel labored for an indeterminate period over how he might get control of the situation on Earth. Then an epiphany struck him. The answer to his dilemma lay before him. After conferring with Luxcius and stirring his anger toward the One he shared his desire to dismantle the One's plans. He would create a civil conflict of the two cultures on Earth. Then Luxcius also realized another way where both would get what they wanted by creating a formidable dilemma in Orion.

Beliel and Luxcius would not stop until they wiped out both cultures on the Earth and end the ridiculous abomination of creation. To accomplish this, they reached into a star system of the Orion constellation. There they found a race of creatures living upon a planet revolving about a binary star called Sirius.

These primates were very similar to Terran in most physical respects. They developed independently of the One and the Djinn. The Atlanteans created high technology developed over several hundred thousand of years. They were a species capable of star travel. They were excellent candidates for their plan of interference in Earth's affairs.

With Beliel's help, the binary star became unstable and produced a deadly radiation that killed all females of their species, leaving the Orion's with no hope of a continuation of their kind. They built interstellar ships to scour the universe for a new home and life that might provide them with new breeding stock. Luxcius made sure they would find Earth in their search for other life.

Beliel knew the Orion presence could bring about the undoing of the cohesive culture of the Atlanteans by causing dissent in the council. It would weaken their potential for a successful war. With the addition of enormous knowledge and mental power at their full potential, the Lemurians could then overwhelm the Atlanteans in a great war bringing them into submission or destroying them. Then after they subdued the remaining Atlanteans to redirect their consciousness away from the One to the way of the Djinn Beliel.

The day the Orions arrived upon the Earth was not without

an exceptional reaction from both the Atlanteans and the Lemurians. Their entry was a dazzling light show meant to impress the Terrans with their power and presence. When the Orions landed, it would be Atlantis that became their first contact. One regional clan called the Baal Tribe welcomed them with open arms. They, too, inclined toward invention and cleverness.

After a careful assessment of both cultures, the Orions surmised the Atlanteans possessed powerful will, but they enjoyed limited mental ability. In contrast, the Lemurians possessed greater mental capacities, but their individual will to be far weaker but socially stronger in their collective.

The similarity of the Lemurian collective appealed to Beliel, though the collective might have proven to be unwieldy and difficult to persuade. After considering their choices, Luxcius suggested that Beliel approach the Atlanteans and sow the dissent against the presence of the Orions. Beliel was confident he could destroy the Atlantean culture through a civil war.

Convincing the Atlanteans through a display of superior power and strength of the Orion technology proved too seductive and simple. Influencing the Lemurians with their telepathic abilities became troublesome, as he expected.

Beliel played both sides on influencing the Atlantean council. He convinced the Atlantean council integration of the Orion technology into the Atlantean culture would insure the Atlantean dominance of the planet. The Atlantean's desire for power and domination forced some of the council to play right into Beliel's hands.

The Orions were quick to display their technological feats, hoping to impress the natives. The Atlanteans did not see this technology as a set of ancillary tools from an advanced race of beings. They believed this 'Teclogi or fierce logic' they referred to be a way of life. This factor would form a strong resistance within the council. After much debate, the responsibility lay finally in the hands of the Baal Tribe.

The Orion's intent was simple. They wanted breeding stock from the tribe and in exchange, the Orions would provide some of their technology with instructions on its use. Since the Atlanteans did not hold their women in high regard, trading them for this new cleverness seemed reasonable. Once the deal struck, the Orions wasted no time. They began genetic manipulations upon the Terran females to bring the Terran species into closer similarity and alignment to their own kind.

Several thousands of years and hundreds of genetic mutations later brought success. The females were ready to breed. The Atlanteans received their cold crystal technology from the Orions as promised and the Baal being clever and innovative, wasted no time to put this new 'Teclogi' into use.

Among their first feats was learning how to make giant crystals. They applied the technology to convert light from the sun into energy and distributed that energy to work around the entire continent. Before long, they integrated it into their society for transportation and communications.

They put a vast network of harmonic energy grids into place inside temples of power on three different mountain peaks devoted to the God Taoi. Using these huge crystals mounted atop the temples and aimed at the sun converted enormous energy, which was stored at the base of each temple. Then the energy transmitted as waves of neutral force across the land.

This force was unlike our electrical energy today. It could only require one line for transmission, but this neutral force energy required no lines because they distributed the energy without wires as a kind of radio wave. Individual needs were met anywhere by tuning into the grids for the required power needed using adjustable smaller crystals.

The knowledge of fundamental forces allowed them to accomplish amazing feats of engineering such as artificial lighting, anti-gravity ships providing aerial travel to expand their borders into other lands, huge sound drilling machines that could easily mine minerals from the Earth, a rudimentary form of television, boats that ran under water like submarines. The Atlanteans would become the first empire builders with outposts stretching out from the mother continent across the globe into and including what is now South America and Mexico.

The Atlanteans learned about power and its value and that they could seize it through aggression. So, fighting became a way of life. They converted some crystals to turn the sun's energy into a destructive ray called the 'Mashmak Tuumak' the ray of fire, a forerunner of the modern-day laser, perhaps. They felt it was their birthright to command the wrath of Taoi upon their enemies of the Earth. The Atlanteans grew hungry to possess other lands and dominate other cultures.

The Lemurians were a constant source of conflict and

Plans Go Further Astray

proved not so easy to dominate. Their powers of mental persuasion developed into their own formidable weapon. They could project illusions into their enemy's mind and control their behavior. Some knew among Atlantean warriors that 'if you meet a Lemurian, cleave his head from his shoulders before he deceives you!'

The behavior of the Atlanteans pleased Beliel. He believed it would only be a matter of time before the Terrans would destroy one another through war, which would become a new and permanent way of life for Terrans.

Meanwhile, the Orions unconcerned for Terran affairs, left the Earth and went off to an area of the Pleadien star cluster. They made a new home there, carrying with them the prized mutated Terran females. They left a skeleton crew of engineers behind to assist the Atlanteans with other applications of their technology. There was little concern for the remaining mutant females left behind. The Atlanteans felt little regard for them.

Considered as freaks, they removed them and pushed them away as outcasts from Atlantean society. The mutants left the principal center of civilization, forming their own colonies in adjacent lands, and these mutant hybrids would form the new Proto-Terran species called Homo-Erectus.

The influence of Teclogi on their culture troubled the Atlantean kings. The dissent in the council of kings grew worse and began a strong rift between tribes until a civil war broke out. They considered those who wanted the old ways the children of the 'Law of the One'. While the others in favor of this change followed the Djinn Belial, known as the 'Children of Beliel'.

Before long, Beliel would achieve his desired goal. The Atlantean princes reapplied the crystal technology to enhance their own genetic structure and advanced their own development beyond a hundred thousand of years of evolution. The princes possessed new psychic powers and compared themselves to the gods, but they still craved the aggressive approach to greater value. They launched a new campaign against the Orions. By adjusting the frequency of the giant crystals, they could bolster their own mental powers, allowing them to reach out over vast regions of space beyond the planet Earth.

They did not know, however, the new frequencies proved destructive to vast underground methane chambers under the continent. Strung along the mantel of the continent, the chambers exploded one day, causing massive collapses and reduced the continent to a series of five islands. The gravitational balance of the Earth suffered anomalies, causing the second moon to plunge into the Earth. The result was violent volcanic reactions with massive widespread earthquakes and five-hundred-foot tidal waves. This caused the submersion of the greater landmass of the eastern and western portions of Gwandana, called Lemuria and Atlantis. The deluge wiped out almost the entire races of Lemuria and Atlantis nearly over-night.

Later, Solon the sage of Greece, discovered the knowledge of the last island that was known in the Egyptian records kept in Alexandria. He then passed the story along to Plato, one of his students, and then Plato described the account in his story,

Plans Go Further Astray

'The Republic.' This last remnant island sank beneath the sea eleven-thousand five-hundred years ago, leaving no trace. We have found only a few relics and artifacts from the outposts of the Yucatan, the mountain peaks of Peru and the shores of the Mediterranean.

Beliel believed they had settled all on Earth and did not realize that the Proto-Terran species still survived. The legends of their mother-continent passed on verbally to their young until lost to antiquity.

A time of approximately 450,000 years ago before the destruction of Atlantis and Lemuria, the twin dwarf star returned along with its six planets and one which was inhabited by a race called the Anu. They were very tall, on average about 9 feet in height. They landed in ships from their planet while near Earth. Their planet was called Nibiru by the Sumerian accounts in their cuneiform clay records. The name meant the 'planet crosser.'

Their atmosphere was slipping away and their technology to keep it intact needed a copious amount of gold. They brought their labor force down to the planet to mine for the mineral using fast smelters.

It was not long before the Gigi (the laborers) complained about the work becoming a burden. King Anu called upon Enki and Isis, their best scientists and geneticists, to solve the problem. The king wanted to create an additional work force by genetically engineering the Homo-Erectus Terrans into semi-intelligent workers who could follow their instructions but not so intelligent to rebel. They grafted Anunnaki blood to the Terran blood of the Homo-Erectus. They changed the brain and spinal cord to limit the life cycle to one hundred years.

When the time came to leave, King Anu left a contingent of Governs to rule over Earth until they returned once again to mine for 'their' gold. While, the king wanted to protect the precious minerals they already mined from other thieves.

These regional monarchs were Yahweh, Krishna, Allah, Vishnu, Ishtar, and Enlil. Anu's other younger son, Enki, was promised a seat over a portion of the land, but he wanted to rule the entire planet. In his insolence to the king, the king gave his seat over to his brother Enlil instead. Enki then killed his brother out of anger. They then banished Enki from the garden E-din. Then he became a nomad and traveled far north to Hyperborea in the land of Nod. Then he returned later and entered the city of Ur. There, the Babylonians revered him and raised up as their deity. He taught them language, science, astronomy and mathematics, and the origins of his home world, Nibiru.

The Anunnaki monarchs discovered the Proto-Terran females from the Orion genetic work. Since the genetic changes for the Orions as concubines, the Anunnaki found them to be beautiful. They copulated with them and married them. Their offspring created a new species of Giants called the great and mighty ones (Titans) which roamed over the lands. [biblical reference, Genesis 6-4 KJV:] "There were giants in the earth in those days; and also, after that, when the sons of God came in unto the daughters of men, and they bare children to them, the same became mighty men which were of old, men of renown."

Initially, the Titans were not a problem. In fact, the Anu monarchs used them for monumental tasks, such as building temples and palaces in their regional lands. This worked very well until the food supply required to feed these monsters ran short. They lost control of the beasts, and the beasts became cannibals and ravaged the countryside all over the world.

As the dwarf star Nemesis came around again, the One became distraught about the conditions on Earth that interfered with her plans. So, she shifted the orbit of Nibiru, bringing it closer to Earth, causing the planet to stop rotating and swung the axis of the Earth 45 degrees off the original axis, causing the great flood.

They did not well know before it, but the greater amount of water of the oceans sits at the equator of the planet by centrifugal force. When the planet stopped rotating and the axis tilted, all that water rushed over the land, wiping almost everything off the surface. It destroyed the Titans and much of the population on the planet by a tidal wave several thousand-feet high.

The One wanted to start over and this would put down the vile and destructive behavior of the Atlanteans, the Lemurians and the Titan after the great flood recedes. The remnants would begin again to unlearn the mistakes of their predecessors. But the battle for Earth had just begun.

These were trying times for the One. The aggressive behavior of her children perplexed her. She wondered if Sukon's light irradiating the planet would guide them to a loving approach to life. Other life on the Earth and their genetic manipulations did not concern her much. She felt the enhancements of human genetic structure from a more advanced life form would only help them assimilate the light from Sukon. The events that followed troubled her. The massive loss of life from the planetary instabilities was regrettable.

The incarnation of new imprints (the children of the fallen) would continue to provide opportunities for those to learn from past mistakes. The Akasha stored the errors in judgment. Losing life seemed appropriate. It was a natural way to clear away the aggressions, giving a fresh start for those that remained. It presented a dramatic turning point in the history of Earth. This would be what the evolutionists would call later natural selection of the most appropriate species. The Proto-Humans that survived the cataclysms and the resulting deluge did not show these aggressive traits and besides there were the remaining Nome-Lu-Lu living deep within the planet whom she cared about the most.

[Note to the reader:] For those who favor prehistory via biblical scripture, the events depicted in Genesis scripture are metaphorical regarding the children of Abra living in Nod. These were the genetic refugees, or the outcasts of Atlantis. They escaped the destruction of Atlantis and Lemuria by going to another land (later known as Hyperborea).

They became the nations of Abra or (Abra-ham) which

translates to "father of all nations." Perhaps the surviving Proto-Humans described by metaphor as the 'Lot' were those chosen for alien breeding and cast out of Atlantis. The story of the destruction is a story symbolic of two evil cities...Sodom and Gomorrah. Is it also perhaps the story of the actual destruction of Atlantis and Lemuria by metaphor, the story of Sodom and Gomorrah? Perhaps this was a way to reflect on a moral about what happens to those who do not follow the law of the One. This was the beginning of the teachings to fear the Most-High God's wrath.

The main issue for the One relates to the unexplained aggressive behavior of the children of the fallen. This disturbed her and was an additional problem that made the fallen rehabilitation more difficult. Aggression was contrary to love and would be a significant stumbling block to their growth. Again, she did not expect this reaction, assuming it was because of higher consciousness mixing with lower animal form vibrations in the third dimension.

Being a Djinn of origin, one would think she would know all, but this was all new in the experience of the One. There was no precedent in her history. The One was the first of Her kind to emerge with love and freedom of expression from a traditional form. She sparked the evolution of new conscious territory in her plane of existence, the upper kingdom of light worlds.

They did not perceive this turn of events as the best of all possibilities. The One questioned her entire approach to existence. By Djinn standards, she was young and having little experience compared to her elders. Her insistence on an alternative approach could also be flawed by arrogance. She was pure of heart. The idea left her with an inescapable conclusion. She might need guidance from those who were more experienced. She knew she would have to humble herself before the Djinn collective if she wanted their help.

The One understood the collective. She knew they did not perceive her approach to be righteous. Bael provided a separate sphere of reality which she could exist in exile beyond the collective. She knew they would gloat when word came to the collective that she would seek the advice of the High Council. The One stood once again before Bael, Arjaxx, and Beliel and the others. Her demeanor was somber and humble. She whispered.

"Great and honorable members of the council. We are here to ask for your guidance. Matters have developed unexpectedly and perhaps our experience falls short of handling it. We felt even though we have differences of opinion, this would not deter you from acknowledging our request."

Bael spoke first.

"Dear young one. We are pleased to view your integrity to acknowledge that you have need. We will hear your petitions. Bael continued. What is the nature of your request?"

The One paused before responding.

"The incongruity of events unfolding in the lower conscious state in the astral vibration manifested by our fallen children troubles us. We have taken certain steps to re-establish order and provide ways to give those who have fallen a path to return. It seems despite trying to bring about harmony in this matter, negative elements continue to arise that work beyond our control and bring greater calamity to the situation."

Beliel couldn't refrain from smiling. Then he chided the One.

"Perhaps calamity does not fall far from its source. Is it not true that this calamity must exist within you, young one? You know of the prime law...all that exists and may exist must come from within thy own being. Perhaps, therefore, you cannot prevent further calamity. This keeps emerging from your core. And let us not forget you emerged from the Praxxis rift. That fact alone speaks for itself."

The One turned to Beliel to respond.

"There is no argument in this. We emerged from the rift of Praxxis. This stands for itself. However, we believe to you and the other distinguished members of the High Council, it is that fact which gives us the unique and independent elements which brings the wonderful changes in our core. This sets us apart from our ancestry. We believe these changes are for good reasons."

"We would hope some sense of understanding might rise out of this and further that you can find good reasons in your core to assist even to one of your kind that is different."

Bael nodded with a brief look of compassion toward the One, Beliel and the others. After there was some muffled discussion amongst the Council members, all attention then turned to Bael for some confirmation of the direction taken.

Beliel then spoke.

"Your demeanor seems humble enough, yet you speak defiantly again about your way! We see you want our help, yet you remain arrogant and defiant. I see no reason to extend…"

Bael leaned forward, raising his hand to gesture the suspension of Beliel's sharp reaction. Then he turned to whisper comments to Beliel on his left while covering his mouth.

Beliel nodded as Bael turned to Arjaxx on his right and continued to whisper to him.

Bael then turned to the One and paused. He offered a gentle but condescending smile as he prefaced their unified decision.

"Well, young one, you must forgive brother Beliel. His zeal is conservative. We will allow your provocative comments. You are young and without the wisdom of diplomacy. You will not find us all together unsympathetic."

The One bowed her head.

"Forgive us this transgression. We did not mean to be disrespectful."

Bael smiled. He nodded to confirm the acceptance of the One's apology. Bael now sat straight, and with some pomp and circumstance, straightened his robes. He stiffened at his pronouncement.

"It is the unanimous opinion of the High Council someone will help the young one. Let it be known to all the High Council is not without some compassion for its own when trouble arises."

Beliel interrupted.

"In fact, it would be my delight to assist you myself. Your situation interests me a great deal. It would be an honor and a pleasure to help you."

Beliel's offer moved the One. She smiled at the Council with joy and happiness about the decision. Strong emotion overwhelmed the One for a moment before she responded.

"It pleased us you will come to our aid. She continued. And we offer gratitude to you, Beliel, for your generous offer."

Beliel smiled with a Cheshire-like grimace while expressing private glee with this outcome. This affords him another opportunity to meddle with the One's affairs. Now he could plot more ways to interfere and undermine her. While, his ambition for the Supreme seat on the Council was all but confirmed.

Later, Beliel walked along with the One and explained.

"You cannot just allow these lower hybrids to run amok. Someone must teach them to live by certain rules of conduct."

The One listened as they walked. Beliel continued.

"These hybrids are unconscious beasts." Then he paused and smiled. Beliel realized he had overstepped his bounds with his judgment and rephrased.

"Well… almost beasts, anyway. And cannot fathom self-responsibility in their unconsciousness state! They need guidelines. They need outer laws to live by. So, they may come to understand the inner law." He placed a firm hand on the One's shoulder, coaxing a desired response.

"You understand, don't you?"

The One gazed downward and nodded. With that minor concession, Beliel moved on.

"But before that, they need to be tested."

The One looked puzzled. "Tested? How? Why?"

Beliel smiled as he tilted his head back with confidence.

"They need to be worthy to receive those laws and the guidance. And above all, their loyalty and allegiance need to be confirmed. Then, they will respect your guidance and come to understand it. Your children are without experience and knowledge. You must rule them with a firm hand. It will be a new tough love you will offer them with firm leadership. They will come to fear and respect you."

Beliel's approach intrigued the One. Beliel's expressed wisdom in the matter seemed captivating. Yet in the One's innocence she could not see the subtle twisting going on in Beliel's tutelage. She was reluctant and concerned about the use of fear, but she was eager to set the fallen straight upon a path of return. Above all, the One was interested in ways to arrest more outbreaks of violence and aggression.

As time passed on Earth, the One tested many for their worthiness and to establish their loyalty and allegiance. The One would have those who would act as emissaries speaking to them using angels to make them prophets of her word. The One gave these prophets visions of the future to help guide the kings ruling her chosen people. She set aside those who would follow her laws and protected them from the onslaught of aggression from other tribes. The One often used Beliel's advice to express aggression and the wrath of punishment to show the chosen that they must obey her laws. She would allow someone to kill if they strayed from her law. Soon the chosen would come to fear Her and obeyed Her.

All of this troubled the One. She wondered where the love

was she expressed in her children? Where was the appreciation for life? There were rules to live by, yes. When those rules are broken, they got punished and even put to death. Yet there seemed to be as much lawlessness and aggression as before. Her chosen loved her yes but out of fear not out of natural devotion. This frustrated her. She realized they did not know Her as She was and still is about... unconditional love, light and compassion.

The One questioned Beliel's approach. She understood that her love for her fallen children turned into something vile and harsh and unloving. She realized Beliel had betrayed her by influencing her to turn against her way. Beliel had convinced the One to create a separation between her and her children. Then it struck the One like a thunderbolt. It must have been his plan...their plan all along...to undermine her way of love, forgiveness, and compassion. Beliel's intention, guided by the others, was to destroy the One's relationship with the fallen and undermine Her ability to bring them back. Then She remembered Luxcius's words; "I will make sure they never return."

The One realized the true nature of this hideous conspiracy against her. She considered who her loyal friends were and where their loyalties lay. She then considered the inevitable...to declare war!

The Confrontation

The One grieved deeply over her situation. The shock and dismay of this terrible betrayal continued to overwhelm her in ever-increasing waves. Never had she felt such powerful feelings. She was trying to embrace the unthinkable. It burned in her heart like an ember, generating tumultuous anger and fury. Beliel had taught her well. He had shown her their way, and it shifted her from great sadness to rage. Her energy turned crimson and shook the whole of her realm as an earthquake of monumental destructive power. All the Stellar Minds turned to acknowledge her intention. For the first time, the One felt her power culminate into an explosive force. Her love and compassion had turned to a great and dark purpose.

Before she could express that dark purpose, she needed to prepare the way so that her purpose would not be cut short. She felt terrible setting this cause in motion, but it seemed the only way afforded to her. She needed to confront the collective with the might of her being to set the situation straight for all eternities.

She dared not think about Beliel and the rage against him. The deepest hurt for the One was that sickly sweet kindness masking the vile intolerance and deceit underneath. That 'kindnesses extended to her like a piece of poisonous candy to a child. What an awful deceit. It was too terrible to conceive. Her innocence was violated, and she felt foolish. But in all her anger, the One did not turn it upon herself. The collective had failed in that. In fact, the One immediately forgave herself for not being able to see it... an effect of her unconditional love.

While her consciousness considered every aspect of the

matter, the One could not stop weeping. She would pause for moments, stepping back to reflect on past events. Then more tears would pour from her. She knew the truth had to be exposed. This terrible darkness caused her being to shudder. She could hardly embrace what she was about to do.

She also discovered something else, realizing something important, making the difference between her and the collective. The One could use great darkness to overcome even more terrible darkness. She realized it could evoke greater light if she remained neutral. The immutable truth: manipulated darkness could create greater light, would become an eternal standard for her. It would stand as a guiding principle for her realm and for all eternities to come. For discovering this truth, she could feel gratefulness toward the collective.

Suddenly, with all her preparations, the One realized the fallen children were in grave danger. There was a fifth column of darkness behind her, lines aligned with this darkness. Luxcius stood at the ready to assist in any way he could to undermine the One. she needed to do something about this immediately.

The One went to the far reaches of the Angelic realm and sought their help. She prefaced her request that she would only ask those who could embrace her way. She stressed that their loyalty to her was imperative and could never to be questioned. Then four angels stepped forward with great enthusiasm for her cause.

Their willingness to help moved her. She then made them her Watchtower Guardians. She placed them at four cardinal points about the Earth, so they might protect the fallen from any harm. These were to be the four Arch Angels: Gabriel, Raphael, Uriel, and Michael. They defined a square about the sphere of the Earth. Within this defense, Luxcius could not invite an alliance with the Djinn to destroy the fallen.

Soon tens of myriads of other angels joined in the One's cause, pledging their willingness to fight the Djinn. The angels were never keen to sympathize with the collective. [note to the reader here:] In our culture, the idea of angels has always been kind, passive, and protective creatures toward the meek and needy. They are swift to act violently with severity. They are good with communications and negotiations but are violent creatures, warriors who were quite vicious in battle. The angels are always carrying swords and always described in scripture as those who carry out the wrath and destruction of God.

The Djinn were tough, quite strong, and almost invincible to attack. The angels possessed unique weapons. These were swords made of Wraithe. Wraithe is a material found only in the realm of the angels. It is so sharp it could prove fatal against Djinn if wielded with cunning and prowess. The Djinn were aware of its existence and mused of its mythological nature. They did not consider it a genuine threat to their existence.

The One remembered those who supported her from the Ursa quadrant. So, she went to Ursa Major to speak with the Council of Nine. She explained to them what had happened and the conspiracy emerging all around her. Afterward, she pleaded for their help in the conflict. As the One arrived upon Ursa Prime, Anodon greeted her.

"Welcome brother, we've been expecting your arrival. We are aware of the situation."

The One smiled and nodded before she spoke.

"There is much to discuss." As they hurried through the courtyard of the palace of Ursa Prime, the One felt relieved to be in supportive surroundings. Down the steps of the palace gate came Deloi the Just and Arinax the Bold. They smiled broadly at the One approaching with Anodon.

Deloi the Just spoke first.

"Greetings, great brother from Praxxis. Please feel at home in our humble abode. We are eager to hear of your exploits since they put your exile into effect." Arinax the Bold added. "Yes. Yes, my brother. We are also eager to know more about the rumors of impending conflict. Please tell us, is this true?" The One sat on a slab of pure white alabaster-like stone. It was different. It was soft and warm to the touch. It appeared to be translucent, capturing the light of many colors around it making it appear like mother-of-pearl. She sighed with relief, feeling its warmth and comfort. She felt and looked weary. The three Djinn huddled around her, placing their hands on her back and shoulders, offering her their comfort and solace. The One began slowly. "Brothers, it is good to see you again. I feel overwhelmed by your hospitality and grace. It has been a long and arduous journey since the High Council handed down their edict. It was only the beginning of our troubles. Now this catastrophe befalls us, we feel we have no choice.

We are to go forward in this just cause. Still, we regret it seems to be the only course of action to take. We feel most disturbed by the unfolding of these events. Beliel is at the root. We are not clear why he has set himself against us, but he has almost single-handedly undermined all our efforts to achieve our goals on the Earth with our fallen ones."

Anodon then spoke. "Brother, you are too kind and perhaps naïve! We have all known for some time that Bael's leadership in the High Council is being challenged. Beliel's ambition for Bael's seat is unquestioned. Clearly his desire to rule the Djinn has made him desperate. Beliel seeks a way to create unrest and to cause doubt about Bael's ability to rule. It seems obvious to us, but perhaps not to you. You have become part of his plan to accomplish just that!"

The One looked perplexed. "We do not understand! What has that to do with us?"

Deloi the Just chimed in. "Brother, your love blinds you even to this truth. Beliel intends to make you the just cause for his plan to undermine Bael's judgment. He intends to prove to the Council his judgment to let you live was wrong. He intends to prove to the Council your love threatens the very heart and fiber of the collective and they should destroy you." The One didn't seem surprised by that news. Although it created a deeper resolve for her conclusions. The expression of her countenance shrunk and became more concentrated. Her mood grew more pensive. Then she turned to her friends. "It's very clear to you why we are here? We desperately need your help and more if you can find it. This may turn to be most unfortunate. But we want to be prepared for the worst before we enter their lair. We have summoned as many of the angelic realm as we could. They're prepared to move against the Djinn as soon as we are ready." The One softened for a moment. Then she turned to Anodon.

"You realize I still hope this can resolve peacefully. We fully intend to approach diplomatically."

Anadon smiled affectionately.

"Oh, sweet brother, for such a loving being you must know we do not know you for your diplomacy!" The One smiled at this remark. "Yes. Yes, we know it. We wish it were different, though."

Anadon continued with a smile. "But You must realize you can be nothing other than what you are… yes?" The One nodded with a smile. "Yes. Of course, you're right, my brother." They stood at the gate of the palace, grasping each other in a loving hug. Deloi the Just spoke kindly to the One. "We are with you, great One. No matter what happens. Trust in what you are doing. It is for the best... for all of us." The others grasped her arms, looking at her with great passion and respect. "May the all-pervading force of life bind us all together, bringing good will to all."

"Brother, Arinax quickly pleaded. You will not go alone, will you?" The One turned and smiled. "Be not afraid for us. Besides, I have an angelic host watching over us." The One left them with lingering fondness in her heart. They're good friends and she cherished their friendship even more now. Her next order of concern was her own children. The Stellar

Minds were the last to prepare for the coming conflict. She went to them, declaring the situation. They were all eager to help and support their mother. She told them to form a great ring around and about the realm of their existence. There would be nothing that could pass this ring. Henceforth, and for all eternities, she would call this the "Ring Pass Not". What had passed asunder shall not pass this boundary. What they do shall never be undone. So let it be said, so let it be done.

The One pointed to the area beyond the boundary formed by her unfallen. "There shall be a neutral zone. If any ancient one shall enter this neutral zone toward our realm, we shall declare it an act of war. And so we shall deal with swiftly and severely, without mercy?" So, it was then the One made ready to approach the Djinn collective. She went straight for the High Council. The time faced Bael and Beliel directly.

Meanwhile, rumors about the One's coming ran rampant throughout the collective like a wildfire.

Bael addressed Beliel in his private chambers. "Beliel, your meddling has brought grave consequences to us all. I believe that the One means to take violent action against you and perhaps against the whole of the collective." Beliel spoke in his defense.

"Brother Bael surely you must realize I did these things to reveal her continued defiance and intended violations of your edict." Bael continued. "Perhaps. She presents an increased threat now. We will have to deal with her differently. You must not come forward if she should call you out. You must remain here, you understand? Your appearance will only make matters worse." Beliel looked frustrated and complained, but stopped.

"As you wish, elder. But I think if I stood beside you, it would make our united stand clear to everyone." Bael replied affirmatively.

"Unity of our position is known. For now, we need to defuse the situation. Your presence will not help." Beliel backed off. "Very well, elder. I will comply."

In that moment, one of Bael's aids entered his chambers. "Sire, she has come, and she has brought many angels with her." Bael looked at Beliel and tightened his lips to brace for the confrontation. Bael emerged into the Hall of the Just and sat down in his seat with Arjaxx at his right. Beliel's vacant seat was obvious. Bael motioned to open the great doors of the hall to allow the One to enter. As the doors opened, four angels entered immediately, two on each side making the way clear for the One to enter. They all approached the center, facing the elders. The rest of the Council gasped to see the angels. We rarely saw them in the collective realm. Angels were a breed, not welcome. The feeling was mutual. The collective did not easily tolerate such a violent race in their midst. They were usually aggressive and menacing.

Bael spoke first. "Greetings young one. To what do we owe this visit?" The One stood firm in her stance, leaning slightly forward with her form bearing only partial exposure to the High Council. her voice broke into a strong and serious tone. "Do not beguile us with your coy nature! You are fully aware of why we are here. We bring charges against the one called Beliel. Bring him forth so he may face these charges." Bael turned a slight smile at the One's attitude and demeanor but carefully evaded her demand. "Why do you bring these creatures with you? They are unpleasantly aggressive and do not reflect the quality of energy in this great hall." The One grew more impatient in her tone. "This hall is supposed to be a Hall of the Just. They are with us to make sure that justice is served! Again, we demand that you produce Beliel to face our charges." Bael visibly squirmed in his seat while the angels moved forward slightly with their claw-like hands on their wraithe swords. Bael continued to avoid the obvious challenge put forth by the One. "Clearly, this is not how to accomplish your goals. We are not armed. Yet you bring these vile creatures into this sacred place armed with a wraithe. We feel no compunction to answer to your charges under such threats and insinuations." The One realized that Bael had no intention of allowing Beliel to come forth. So, she continued with Bael and the rest of the Council.

"You seem to forget we are of the Djinn. We are aware of your abilities and their capacity to inflict damage and destruction. So, we will place these charges with you and the rest of the council. We hold Beliel and all those who would harbor and assist him and his kind, meaning you and the High Council. You handle deliberate interference with our realm and all its concerns. You seek to undermine the rehabilitation of our fallen ones and aid with their misguidance and the insidious betrayal of our trust and confidence in these matters.

The Confrontation

Therefore, we hold these truths to be self-evident. We declare a 'state of readiness for war' against all Djinn and their sovereigns should they approach and enter the zone of neutrality toward our realm."

Bael looked stunned, but he recovered quickly. "Young one, we see no reason to feel that your charges have merit. Why can't we set down like civilized beings to work this out?" The One turned to walk away. Angels fell in behind her to cover as her rear guard. The One spoke while still walking away. "We will not remain here to hear more of your treachery. Our desire to talk with you has ended. Your refusal to allow Beliel to face our charges and trial is a clear sign of your continued deceit! Now, with greater integrity than you have provided us, we will state our intentions plainly. If you cross our neutral zone, we consider that action an act of war. We will deal with you swiftly and sternly. We shall be determined that further assaults upon your realms will continue until we settle."

The One passed through the great doors of the Hall of the Just, closing them abruptly behind her. Arjaxx turned to Bael for his response to the One's outburst and violent declaration. "Brother, do you think she is serious about this declaration of war?"

Bael answered solemnly. "Apparently, we have no choice but to take her seriously. We have no choice but to lay siege upon her realm immediately. We must eliminate this pestilence once and for all."

At the Second Knot of Altair, thousands of angels appeared with several Djinn near the One's neutral zone. Two Stellar Minds guarded this part of the ring, standing at the ready.

Djinn crossed into the neutral zone with thousands of angels leading; confident they could break through the ring. They saw only two of the One's children standing guard. Then it startled them to see thousands of armed angels suddenly appear behind the children. Some angelic tribes could control light passing through them, giving them the power of invisibility at will.

The Djinn stopped to consider the odds after seeing them appear. But even though the odds were better balanced, it did not deter them from continuing with their assault into the One's realm.

The angels standing behind the Stellar Minds twitched with anticipation. They could not wait for the Djinn's angels to approach. They leaped out in front and engaged violently with the other tribes. As swords clanked together, the metal-like substance rang differently than an Earth exchange of swords. The wraithe, when struck by another wraithe, produces a shrill high-pitched ringing sound that would be unbearable to hear. Imagine several thousand swords ringing at the same time. It would make your bones shudder.

The first battle seemed longer, though both sides wanted this exchange to be the end. The angels were tough and difficult to kill even with wraithe swords. But the other tribes knew there was only one weapon that could keep an angel from coming back. Their heart had to be extracted from their chest. The best tool for this was a 'Hroke-Crux,' or impaling stake. All angel tribes carried Hroke-Crux into battle. Once an angel was wounded, one or more of their opponents would impale the wounded angel through the heart until the heart came out of the thorax harpooned on the end of the stake. Then, they would jam the stake into the ground, suspending the angel upon its back arched over the stake for all to see. This insured no recovery and certain death for the angel. The battle of the Knot of Altair proved to be more of a slaughter. The forces of the collective began their siege with an overwhelming victory. It was a pitiful sight. So many angels pronged into the surface of the planet Oath Prime, orbiting below its star, Altair. The Djinn intended this battle to be a demoralizing blow, hoping that the conflict would end there. They underestimated the One's resolve to battle until the undeniable conclusion. (Note to the reader:) There are many angelic tribes in the firmament. They exist throughout many quadrants, like the buffalo existed in the great plains of America. Each tribe differed. Overall, they were very tall creatures with broad shoulders, long torsos, and longer limbs. Many could fly even without wings. There were none with feathers. I gave this human trait to them because of their heavenly origins.

They all bore a thick swath of hair-like fur which ran down their backside like the mane of a horse. The fur also continued to grow over and down the front of the head to the upper part of their nostrils, like a widow's peak. Their eye sockets were deep and bony, which created a dark-like shadow around their deep-set eyes. Their eyes were a yellowish color with large black oblong pupils much like a deer's eyes. The Native North Americans, who comprised many tribes, often disliked one another. So, it was with the angels. There were many who did not get along. So, it was easy to find those who would fight against their own kind. The Djinn are immortal. This means they cannot experience death in the normal human concept of mortality. The reason is the immortal fire of their being, also known as the ineffable flame, and stored in their Holy Tabernacle. As long as the flame burns, their life remains unaffected for eternity. If the flame should go out or it is extinguished, then that extinguishes their life cycle permanently. Their flame burns like no fire as humans would understand it. It is a fire, perhaps in the metaphorical sense, but not the common quality of fire burning from some combustible material. Like the sun, it burns unto itself and will not extinguish as a normal fire might when the combustible is exhausted. They can destroy a Djinn body in the interim, but they regenerate a new body out of the ineffable flame. So, the eternal life of Djinn continues through regeneration. The Tabernacle is a sanctuary for all Djinn. Their only vulnerability rests on the exposure of the Tabernacle to any outside presence or force which could threaten the flame of any Djinn. The location of the Tabernacle is kept secret and known only to the Djinn. They deny access to any creature other than Djinn. A Djinn emerges as a mortal at first after confirmation by the collective High Council becomes eternal. Their individual flame begins and set into place in the Tabernacle, never to be disturbed again for all eternities. Each flame is a unique quality of vibration for each Djinn. It is also like the vibration of their realm. Should their flame cease to burn, then they, along with their realm and everything in it, would cease to exist? One belief is the ancient ones that live in heaven before the times of the One are all immortal. Many of the ancient ones live long lives. They live thousands of

War Breaks Out

years by earth standards, but they are not immortal by nature. Perhaps one might think the human life span of 100 years compared to tens of thousands of years might appear as immortal. We believe it the angelic tribes to be immortal, but they are not. They live long lives unless cut short by the forcible removal of their heart from their body. The Djinn are immortal by nature, but they are not unique in that way. There are other beings in the firmament which are also immortal, but their story goes beyond this work. The slaughter of angels and the Stellar Minds at the Second Knot of Altair made a powerful impact on the angelic tribes and the One. The One's immortality provided the restoration of the Stellar Minds, mortally wounded in battle not long after the conflict. Angels who lost their lives were lost permanently. The One was grateful for their sacrifice and held a memorial in their honor. While at that place, she vowed to learn from that terrible experience and would aggressively seek to minimize future losses. The battles continued to ensue thereafter, with both sides fighting ferociously. The numbers of losses on both sides were great but more dispersed. Beliel became concerned. The military strategy of the One proved to be more formidable than expected. He often expressed his frustration to Arjaxx and Bael. Though the angelic tribes continued to fight for the Djinns, their morale waned. Beliel grew impatient about the war. He felt desperate to change the tide of the war quickly. Then, in a sinister and merciless move, he perceived how he could end the war quickly. He went to Arjaxx first, suggesting a clandestine operation to break into the sanctuary of the Tabernacle. He wanted to put out the flame of the One before anyone was the wiser. At first, Arjaxx was shocked and repulsed that Beliel would consider such an awful act. After many more angelic losses, Arjaxx soon agreed with the idea. Arjaxx agreed to approach Bael along with Beliel to bolster support for the idea. Bael was in his chambers, reviewing reports from the battles raging on many fronts.

Arjaxx entered first.

"Sire, I've come with Beliel to suggest a plan to end the war quickly." Bael's eyes widened. He stood up, placing his hands behind himself, still staring at the battle reports. "I'm listening." Arjaxx referred to Beliel's basic plan because he knew how Bael would feel. "Beliel has conceived of a plan to raid the Tabernacle and destroy the One's flame, sire." Beliel chimed in. "You're Excellency, I feel this is an expedient way to prevent further losses which allows you to reverse your decision about the young one with honor." Bael turned, walking away from both, saying nothing to this. Then he turned again to face Beliel. "You'd like that, wouldn't you?"

Beliel bowed his head and responded. "Well, I am trying to look out for your welfare, sire."

Bael looked him straight in the eye. "It's a terrible thing you are asking. So, it has come to this! For the sake of expediency, we will extinguish one of our brothers while violating another prime directive...the sanctuary stands for all eternities and shall be inviolate for all. You are setting up a terrible precedent, Beliel. Where will this end? I wonder? I fear the outcome of this conflict will not go well. The fabric of the collective is being torn asunder."

Arjaxx added. "Sire, even though this is a terrible act, we can end this conflict with her presence gone. Then we can restore our cherished traditions. No one must know of our deeds. It will be easy to accomplish. None ever needs to guard the sanctuary. So, we can slip in unseen with the deed done in an instant." Bael responded to Arjaxx sternly. "Dear brother. Do not be so hasty with the clear ease of this plan. May I remind you they do not guard the sanctuary because of the integrity of our prime directive and our desire to hold those directives sacred?" Beliel continued to push to implement his plan. He knew this would be the last act that could seal Bael's political fate with the collective. Beliel continued.

"Excellency, try to consider and weigh the consequences of a prolonged campaign against the One. It behooves us to implement this plan now while we still hold an upper edge of surprise. I'm sure once she is gone, her forces will lose the will to fight and then it will be easy. Our tasks will only involve cleanup operations. We can restore order after that." Bael's expression became pensive. "Well, you may let this deed unfold, but I wash my hands of it. If it goes badly for you, I will not support any agreement to it publicly and I will disavow any complicity in its design." Arjaxx and Beliel smiled and replied.

"We understand, sire." Beliel and Arjaxx appeared at the Tabernacle entrance. As they surmised, no one was present to witness their sinister act. Even though they were alone there, they behaved as though someone was watching. They checked their surroundings, looking over their shoulder to make sure no one would see what they were about to do. The Tabernacle had three concentric chambers. They lined the inner most chamber walls with thousands of elongated glass-like flutes illuminated with the ineffable flames of their brethren. The flames remained intact so long as the flute remained in its vessel. Once removed, the flame cannot be recovered. The feeling inside the chamber was somber, thick with the energy of the collective's essence. Arjaxx was nervous and chided Beliel to be quick. To their combined surprise, they could not find the One's flute or vessel. The One suspected their evil intentions. Disappointed, Beliel and Arjaxx returned to Bael's chamber. Bael patiently waited for the news. "Sire, she has taken her flame away from the Tabernacle. We could not find it." Bael replied with a slight smile and with some respect for the young one. "So, it seems she is cleverer than you expected. Either there is a spy among us, or she has some unusual way of learning of our plan. We must be more cautious."

Meanwhile, in the One's camp, one of her angels reported to her of the Djinn trying to destroy her flame. The One sat down in astonishment. She could not believe her brothers were so desperate. She believed they would not resort to such an evil act of destroying her. Some angels had used their telepathic powers to realize the Djinn plan long before they put it into action.

The One knew she needed to take her flame away for safekeeping. But where would she keep it? Then she realized the last place they would think of searching was the Earth. She went to Earth and found Moses and his brother Aaron a chief priest. She knew the Anunnaki overseer, Yahweh influenced Moses. So, she pretended to be Yahweh to communicate with Aaron.

She requested Aaron to build a Tabernacle for 'god' (speaking as Yahweh) on the Earth. Also, Aron was to construct an Ark to contain the Yahweh covenant. The ark would be a suitable device to embrace the One's ineffable flame of her being together with the tablets of laws. Moses spent years engraving the Hebrew letters into the stones which Yahweh gave him earlier.

Then Aaron built the Ark as per her instructions. They restricted access to the Ark to anyone other than Aaron for a short time. The construction was made of chetrum wood and covered with layers of gold, making a powerful, charged capacitor capable of killing anyone who tried to open it. The One kept her flute in the Ark inside the Tabernacle and bade the devoted priest Aaron to watch over and care for them as High Priest of the Tabernacle.

[note to the reader:] Later on, Jehovah the overlord guided the priesthood to use the ark as a weapon to strike down their enemies declaring their 'god' as the one 'god'. Scriptures reported in the Old Testament, powerful bolts of lightning sprang forth from the box, laying waste to thousands of warriors. The One had removed her flute from the ark long before this.

Samuel 6-19: And he smote the men of Bethshemesh, because they had investigated the ark of the Lord, even he smote of the people fifty thousand and threescore and ten men: and the people lamented, because the Lord had smitten [many] of the people with a great slaughter.

There would be one last and final battle. Though it took place on all fronts, including the Earth, it culminated in a place near the Garnet star of Cepheus, on a planet called Ahm-Magi Prime.

[Note to the reader:] it is believed this was the true origin of the derivation of the 'battle of Armageddon', as written in the visions of the Apocalypse by John.] Myriads of angels faced the others standing beside Beliel and Arjaxx while the One stood with her Myriads of angels facing Beliel on the Mount of Procyon, a mountain peak to the west of the plain of Meget, on Ahm-Magi Prime.

Beliel raised his hands outstretched as a signal to his armies in readiness to lay siege against the One and her armies. He spoke one last time before giving the last signal. "Well, young one, we finally meet here to end this debacle."

The One paused before she spoke. "Beliel! she yelled. You do not want to do this. Let it end here, while you still survive!" Beliel laughed at her. "Little one, you are outnumbered and outclassed here. We will smash you into these rocks and do away with your flame when we find where you have hidden it."

"Beliel and Arjaxx! she yelled again. If you charge upon us, we will end your existence here!"

With that statement, she held high above her the flutes of both Beliel and Arjaxx. Beliel looked shocked by this. Arjaxx turned to Beliel and proclaimed, "Sire, I have no desire to die here today. Yield to her, for she holds our life in her hands." Beliel hardened his expression while grimacing at the One. Then he turned to Arjaxx. "You have no courage, Arjaxx. Besides, I think you overestimate her chances." Then he turned back to the One to respond. "You would not dare to end a Djinn's life. It is sacrilege! We know you for your love and compassion. We believe you cannot and will not do this terrible thing. It is not within your being."

"Beliel!" The One yelled for a third time. Your actions have set a terrible cause in motion for us to do terrible things as of late. We will not hesitate to end your lives here and now!" Arjaxx pleaded with Beliel.

"Sire! I think she means to do it!" Beliel turned to Arjaxx

with anger.

"Arjaxx, step aside, if you do not have the courage to go against this little Djinn of no consequence."

At that point, Beliel dropped his arms to signal the charge. The angels on his side ran ahead in a mad dash for battle. Beliel marched forward, making his way to the One. The One raised her right hand and smashed the flute with its vessel of flame on the rocks below. A great shock wave went from that place, rippling through all the eternities. Beliel let out a scream, and his last death rattle for all to hear and see. He dissolved before his armies and his enemies in a blinding flash of crimson light.

The One roared.

"Let all to see the dragon is dead!"

Then, without hesitation, she raised her left hand and spoke.

"Let all to see. The dragon's consort is dead as well." But before she could throw down Arjaxx's flute, Arjaxx cried out. "Wait! Oh, great and merciful Queen. I beg of you, let this end here! For it was Beliel's intention and his awful fate. But it is not my intention." Then Arjaxx raised his arms and issued from his hand a great thunderbolt came forth. "Hold! Cease this conflict at once! I command it, by the right and authority of the Supreme High Council, the will of Bael be done." The angels stopped their charge, and a silence fell upon the strange land. Arjaxx and his angel armies retreated.

"Let us call a truce upon this ground." Arjaxx said to the One. And the One agreed.

Meanwhile, on the Earth high above the mid heavens of the Astral plane, a battle between Luxcius and his angels engaged with Michael and Raphael, while Uriel and Gabriel engaged at the other cardinal points defending the last perimeter. Other angels had joined them to defeat the fifth column before they could reach the holy tabernacle guarded by Aaron. Luxcius learned of the presence of the One's flute and vessel laying there. Luxcius meant to destroy it if he could.

Gabriel warned Aaron about the coming attack before Luxcius approached. He had the Ark of the Covenant removed and taken to a lower cave beneath the Tabernacle in case the perimeter is breached. Just as Michael brought down and wounded Luxcius, the One appeared.

"Hold Arch Angel Michael. Do not destroy my wayward child yet."

"The Great War has ended. There is to be a truce. The great dragon, Beliel, is dead!"

Luxcius cried out to his mother. "How can this be? He is immortal. He cannot be destroyed!"

The One replied. "Oh yes, my child, he is gone forever. For we have slain him by destroying his ineffable flame. He lives no more!" Luxcius wept as his body fell limp upon the earth. The One placed her hand on his head as she whispered. "Why do you weep, my son? He was a betrayer of the truth and defiled all things good and holy. He was an abomination in a holy place, and he misled you, leading you astray from the light for his own sake. It is better you weep for yourself." Luxcius looked up at the One, continuing to weep and sob. "Mother, why have you abandoned me? I was only trying to help."

The One replied. "Luxcius, the dragon, betrayed us. Our love and naivete blinded us and kept us from seeing Beliel's treachery. Your ambition blinded you to his treachery and ambition also when he tempted our children to lust after something beyond them. He hid the truth from them...though they possessed it inside all along. He made them think they were less than they were. You helped separate them even more from the truth and endangered them almost beyond our help. We don't want to harm you. You need to learn and grow to understand the nature of these deeds. We want you to stay here on the Earth and contemplate your actions, my son, and perhaps you will lose your anger against us. Eventually you'll come to understand."

Luxcius said nothing to this but grumbled. "So, there is no mercy for me!" The One responded to this. "The mercy you receive from us will be in your rehabilitation when you return to the light." The One withdrew from the Earth. Behind her were the sounds of Luxcius's cries and growling against her. She instructed her most trusted arch angels Gabriel, Raphael, Uriel, and Michael to remain at their cardinal stations as watchers about the Earth keeping vigilance over Luxcius and the rest of his angels that are bound to Earth with him.

The Truce

The One returned to her place of origin, the Archway of Praxxis. There were two angels and two of her Stellar Minds standing behind her. The Stellar Mind Aihus stood on her right with Methuziel holding the One's flute and vessel she retrieved from the high priest Aaron on Earth. On her left side stood the Stellar Mind Enguz and the angel Theoziel guarding her back and at the ready with his hand gripping a wraithe sword.

For so many Djinns, this place proved to be a thorn in their side. They would always know it not only for its turbulence but also for the emergence of the being that brought turmoil and tumultuous change to their existence. For the One, it was a place of solitude and comfort. The powerful energies splashing violently there quieted her restlessness while the deafening roar softened her pain from the events that unfolded in the war. She felt saddened by the demise of Beliel. It's a shame, she thought to herself, that such a being of his knowledge and experience should have to die. She lamented. If only he could've seen the error of his ways. Then she stopped her thoughts. She learned from this horrible but necessary experience lamenting over that which is lost serves no purpose. She needed to move on. There was much to do and much to rebuild. First, she needed to go to the High Council to establish terms for a truce. Then she needed to consider how she would change her approach to the lost and fallen upon the Earth. The One realized too late her actions on the Earth created a lot of collateral damage while carrying out Beliel's guidance on her fallen. She knew she needed to bring a different message to her children now. She needed to

re-establish the foundation and meaning of her existence on Earth and the all-pervading force of her unconditional love and compassion. There would be no more vengeance and no more wrath and punishment. There would be a new and simple way to replace the old laws Yahweh had given to Moses. This would be dealt with later. For now, she needed to restore her ineffable flame back to its rightful [place in the Holy Tabernacle. With that done, she would once again go to the High Council. The great doors of the Hall of the Just swung open to allow the One and her guardian angels to enter. They approached the High Council, moving along the grand foyer leading to the Supreme Chancellor's seat and the new Right Deputy Chancellor's seat occupied now by Arjaxx. The second seat Beliel had occupied was empty. It was a way that Djinn mourned their loss. In this moment, the atmosphere was tense. Arjaxx grew eager to see the One approaching them. His memory of that terrible moment of Beliel's demise was still present in his consciousness. Then Bael reached out,
placing his hand on Arjaxx's arm, offering him some solace and reassurance. Bael spoke first. "Shall we bid you welcome, young Queen? With your actions, you have made your point to us. With your valor and courage, you've earned the right to call yourself Queen. It is unfortunate that Beliel could not give fealty. Yet we must extend to you also some sense of gratitude. We now understand the extent of his treacherous plan. So, our seats that oversee this prestigious group of distinguished and honorable leaders of the great collective are secured because of your efforts to establish your boundaries."

Meanwhile, on the Earth, the tribes of Abra spread out and developed into many nations. Only those tribes that were significant with the One's interactions along with the activities of the children of the fallen-on Earth are discussed.

Yahwey provided an outer law to Hammurabi, one who ruled Babylonia, or Shinar, as they also knew it. The One told Sukon to continue streaming her way upon the Earth from the solar orb. Historically, Hammurabi attributes the gift of his code of conduct to the sun God Shamash. Later, the One came to know of an effort in Babylon to join Yahwey in heaven, by building a monstrous temple called a Ziggurat. The One came to the Earth to see this monument of pride and arrogance. When She saw what they were doing, she had to hold back her frustration for their lack of understanding and selfish pride. Rather than allow Yahweh's influence, she put a stop to it by creating confusion amongst its builders until the construction stopped all together. [Note to the reader:] In the biblical reference, the Tower of Babel, a multi-layered temple constructed to physically reach heaven with the purpose to join or be with 'God' was defeated by causing all the inhabitants to speak different languages. Here, the key word is Babel when translated, means confusion. There has been no archeological evidence of such a structure in the city of Ur. Offering the benefit of doubt may be because of the poor quality of the building materials, meaning the mud brick used in that day would not have survived the erosion of time. Many nations fought and defeated by other nations following Beliel's pattern of influence; using the act of war to settle differences. There was another instance where the One tried to bring higher knowledge to her children through Sukon's solar orb. In ancient Egypt, during the 18th dynasty, a Pharaoh ascended the throne in 1352 BC called Amenhotep IV. Later he took the name of Akhenaten. Historians know him for toppling the priesthood and demolishing all the temples of Amun in favor of temples erected to his vision of Aten, a monotheistic god of the sun. His unusual and unpopular proclamation that there was only one God for all men came from the light of the sun. His reign was brief. He lived only 16 years. After his violent death, the priesthood reinstated the temples to their original gods. After the Romans invaded and occupied Jerusalem, they set the stage for the One's next move on Earth...the entry of an emissary to offer her teachings of truth. She hoped might lead her children of the fallen to freedom.

The One responded. "Your generosity and wisdom is noted, supreme chancellor. Yes. It's unfortunate that Beliel could not yield. We regret those circumstances that brought him to such misfortune. Yet, we look ahead and shall learn from this a new way for both of us. "We come to elaborate the nature and terms of the truce between Us. With that, it is hoped we can learn to live side by side in our different ways but in harmony while developing a respect for each other and our different ways of existence." Bael smiled and responded nervously about the terms. "We agree, young Queen. So let us discuss the terms." The One began.

"First, let us say from this moment forward we both agree

that the sanctuary of the Tabernacle will never be violated again for all eternities. We shall afore swear it. Second, that we or you shall not violate the truce by violence without some manner of preliminary negotiations to work out any differences between us. We shall afore swear it. Third, that you or any of yours shall not interfere in or by association to anyone may interfere in any matters of our realm, including that region of the Astral level of consciousness called Earth. Shall you afore swear these things?"

Bael leaned over to Arjaxx for a moment to whisper the considerations to these conditions. Arjaxx nodded in agreement. Bael then commented.

"We feel the last of your terms is not without some questions. By your own declarations do you now remove the right of free will of your fallen children to have the freedom to choose their own way? Is it true then you have rescinded the basis for your way as a Djinn? Not unlike us then you will rule your children as we do our kind?" The One realized they caught her in a dilemma. She was honor bound to support and respect her way of complete freedom and free will which leaves her children vulnerable to the wiles and cleverness of the Djinn.

The One responded.

"You're right. Yet, our fallen are without sufficient consciousness to make such choices!" Bael retorted. "Perhaps. But is it not true some of your wisdom still lies within their consciousness? So, they have an equal chance to choose your way or ours... Yes? This would be fair and fair!" The One bowed her head. She knew they could not undo this trap without also undoing the heart of her approach. She knew she would have to concede on this point.

"Very well. We shall concede this point and allow your influence over those who have fallen and live upon the earth, but only if they choose it and only if they invite you! Do you afore swear it?" Bael responded, smiling. "We afore swear it! So let it be said, so let it be done!"

The One responded in like manner. "We also afore swear it! So, let it be said, and so let it be done!" At that moment, the One turned to her guardian angels, nodding in confirmation. Both angels reluctantly withdrew their wraithe swords and placed them in a cross one over the other upon the floor of the great Hall of the Just. This symbolized and completed the truce now in effect. Later, the swords would be placed still in their same arrangement into a crystalline container and displayed at the entrance of the great Hall of the Just for all to see.

Though this seemed an important logical next step for her children, the war in heaven would continue. It would not be with the blood of angels but fought in the uncertain field of her Children's heart where lies are truth and truth are lies. They would fight it on the anvil of the human will and the doubt-filled plane of the human mind. It would be a hostile war where the Earth represented the pivotal jewel for which the forces of light and the forces of darkness would wage their differences to assuage the human heart of her children to swing from the allegiance to the One over to the realm of the

Djinn. The Djinn would not dare to break the covenant with the One not directly, anyway. They would seek to undermine her flock by playing with their illusions and delusions inside their minds, tricking them into thinking their plight is from a cruel and angry God. Their perception of a god's will be rigid administering punishment for an anguish filled life of agony and suffering and for disloyalty and a lack of faith. Through Luxcius, they would cause the children of the fallen to doubt their direction and their heart. They would deceive them to think these forces are unreal and imaginary. It will cause them to turn from the true nature of their spiritual heritage and believe only in the reality of physical life on the Earth.

Problems upon the Earth would remain a nemesis for the One. Issues were many and difficult to resolve without creating additional problems. The fallen state froze compared to their original fluid state.

The physical consciousness within the children of the fallen, called their imprints, culled out from the akashic records. These are trace aspects and essences of the original fallen. With each incarnation, imprints are shaped through the genetic history of parenting structures known as life patterns. Their physical form develops during the gestation period with influences from star patterns, thought forms from the mid-heaven and the Akashic records of previous incarnational experiences.

This was the One's original plan of salvation for the fallen since the separation and polarization of their androgynous nature. The imprint's purpose was to live life and create experience based upon the awareness within while witnessing and learning from what was created. By comparison, the response of the Stellar Mind upon reality was instantaneous. The imprint possessed an inherent delay between what was their internal reality and what they then manifested. This meant time would become a measure of the delay in creating reality on Earth. This delay was variable and could be longer or shorter for everyone.

This delay in manifestation presented an interesting and troublesome quality. In effect, the imprint became a virtual time traveler. As the variable time delay changed reality, it offered infinite possibilities, along with an infinite number of timelines. The imprint's relationship to those realities depended upon the quickness of how it reacted to the truth of its relationship to those realities it created. The imprint is dreaming its world, but it does not know that as a fact. Further, it can unconsciously shift its presence within the dream at random. This shifting happens at a rate that is far too fast for the awareness of the imprint to realize. As changes occur, it incorporates the changes into the dream sequence. So, the imprint detects no gap in the stream of its awareness. The dream construct is based upon several factors; thought processes, emotional states, and memories. So, the world becomes a matrix of these constructs. The psychologist Carl Jung once suggested that a collective unconscious stream of awareness exists below the conscious level. That awareness exists while it agrees with certain common elements in everyone's dreams. This is because of the ancient collective streams of consciousness are connected and left over from the original unified state. This was the hope and saving grace reflected on the plight of the fallen and their deliberate disintegration of consciousness. The fact we are dreaming our reality and unaware of it makes learning any truth about our reality problematic. Dreams are not real. That means our lives are not real also! This is a very disconcerting thought. It is disturbing to consider. What does that mean about life? What does that mean about our reason for being here, and so on? In the present-day experience of human beings, humans are asking those questions that have no answers, such as, who are we? Where did we come from? What are we doing here? How long have we got to live? And where are we going? These questions make up the foundation and enigmatic quality presented in all the philosophies and religions on the Earth. Even the most respected literary volume, the Bible, attempts to reflect on humankind's condition and relationship to spirit through allegory, metaphor and stories of people and their interactions with spirit. The Biblical scriptures are a compilation of accounts adapted from the history of the Chaldean/Babylonian empire during the captivity of the tribe of Judah.

This 'sacred volume' is supposed to be the word of 'God', but it is fragmented and often contradictory, which shows possible extensive editing of the content that occurred. (The main alterations occurred during the ecumenical conference of Mycenae in the 4th century as demanded by Alexander thegreat)

The stories of human drama and interactions with deities often displayed incongruous activities from these spiritual beings. Their reactions did not reflect the properties of humility and compassion expected from higher beings from heaven. Perhaps these stories are about 'the gods' who landed here from another world. The expectation of an advanced species to be as 'Gods' was true to those on earth simply because they came from heaven! Even Jehovah said he was a jealous God and there would be no other gods before him. They expressed all the well know human frailties of anger, hatred, and jealousy.

In man's awake dream world, apart from the dreams within dreams occurring during sleep, are masked imbedded beliefs, legends and myths that sit quietly in the background. These beliefs provide a sense of comfort or cushion to an otherwise scary place. These beliefs add a measure of safety against the unknown or the void. The same way a child insists on having the light kept on chasing away demons secretly waiting to pounce upon them in the darkness. Dreams at night can be nightmares. When the awake dreams of life become nightmares, people seek the help of those specialized in the realm of the spiritual. The churches and their teachers/shepherds try to help mend these afflictions with preaching. There is hope for a better life, either in this world or the next.

    The spiritual doctrine of the 'soul' is a relatively new belief in the modern western world. It has its roots in the texts of the Indo-Aryan and Judeo-Christian cultural dogma. Truths brought here by the One to assist the children of the fallen in their struggle to awaken. Those truths are altered or changed here! So, to awaken the sleeper falls short of the mark through misinterpretation, loss of translations, and or deliberate misguidance. When the One sends information to the fallen, it must pass through layers of consciousness from her level on the (7th dimension) down to the (3rd dimension). Remember, there are at least four levels of increasing density of consciousness between the One's realm and here. If we take the example of light passing through different densities of material such as glass, crystals, or water, it makes objects sharing the two densities appear bent. Visualize, as an example, to place a stick into a shallow pond. The light passing through the water offers the appearance that the stick is bent where the boundary occurs between the air and the water. Now imagine the 'bent' nature of concepts as they pass through greater densities of consciousness. The same thing happens. The difference here is when the information gets bent, it means they lose something in the translation across the 'density boundaries' from the One to here. Many concepts are then sent to those bearing the 'gift' of clairvoyance, (to see visions,) or clairaudience, (to hear voices,) like a kind of psychic intuition, or as some would call a 'hunch'. These abilities can emerge in people who have previous psychic experiences in lives before. They develop those skills through hard work and practice, then they appear as gifts in the present life. This is how the One circumvents the problem of density because the information goes straight to the heart of the gifted one.

By bypassing their mind first. In the past, these special people were 'the anointed' from 'God', as prophets, seers, and mediums. King David often sought the advice of his priesthood, who conveyed messages to him from their god Jehovah. There are many examples of these people in Biblical scripture. The modern-day version of this is the 'Channeler' or 'spirit medium' of spiritual messages. This ability makes possible the breach of the veil between the spirit world and the physical world. This direct contact can often eliminate much of the distortion, even though personal weakness can always present the opportunity for the mind to bend the information given to suit personal needs. [Note to the reader:] Channeled messages are vulnerable to distortion. It requires discipline and training to communicate with the spirit world. Ill health can often arise over time without this training and preparation. Scrutiny and healthy skepticism are important qualities when dealing with disembodied spirits. The ego must be strong, while strong egos can project personal filters that are often applied during the reception of such material by the channeler. The best advice is to use one's own ability to scrutinize the information as to its usefulness in life. By experience, the best form of this gift comes from those who are in a full trance during the communication. This means that the medium's consciousness is asleep while the 'entity' has full control of the medium's faculties. This eliminates the personal filtering. In the other case, the medium is partially awake and is fully aware of what they said and can be altered through the desires of the medium. Since the children of the fallen are dreaming all the time, even when they think they are awake, almost anything can influence and alter their consciousness. Since they are unaware of their input to their dreams means they are susceptible to outside influence. Luxcius's plan is to further undermine the fallen children through the influence of doubt within their minds. This is nothing less than sinister! Doubt needs a vehicle.

    The primary vehicle used here is fear. When the children of the fallen feel fear, there is a desire to defend or protect everything in and around them. They placed doubt within the fear so they will not trust themselves to protect and preserve themselves, or those around them they care about. We also applied the doubt to other matters, like the fear of life. Is it safe or not? Can calamity be prevented? Can happiness be attained? Are all those here meant to suffer? Religionists say yes! When there is atonement for sins and there is achieved an acceptable level of excellent performance (good deeds), then happiness is deserved and granted. This is a fallacy! There are many good people who perform good deeds and are beset by many calamities. But that raises more doubt. These ideas have been superimposed upon us by dark forces to eliminate the possibility of our rising out of our plight to return to our rightful place in the scheme of things.

The crux of the matter has to do with confidence. The sense of self-esteem is in question here. It is being undermined. It makes one to feel they are not 'good' enough or worthy enough in their essence to stand and be counted. Normally, the role of the children of the fallen would be to awaken to the truth of their origins, their purpose... the expression and continuation of the One's unconditional love and compassion would then become something of paramount importance here on Earth and in the rest of her realm. Here extends her realm at the Astral level of consciousness. The Earth and its inhabitants are the remnant of the fallen and need to realize their true condition so they could escape this prison. Rising to overcome it means to challenge the lies and seek the obvious truth of this 'so called' reality. How does one explain to someone who is in prison, but is dreaming their freedom and does not know or believe they are a prisoner? I would say whatever is said would be in question because of doubt! This is not a new thought. Many spiritual teachers have come along offering various approaches to achieve that.

The appeal here is to thwart the doubt by suggesting that

there is a quality within the prisoner that is special, or holy and can connect the prisoner to the hope of a reality of his true freedom. Property is called the 'soul'. Then the church (the prison chaplain) must have its way and suggests the soul needs to be saved. This is not true! It is simply a tool of gathered experience (the imprint) which is guided to retrieve what we have lost in the mud of this dream.

You might say the fallen consciousness was snagged by the fascination of density like a substance misuse, becoming numb to the harshness of their addictive plight. While under the 'drug' of reduced consciousness, each imprint rallies around the fantasies of what might have been while looking to satisfy the hunger for what is missing. The nature of the children of the fallen's behavior is to achieve some measure of success through the gaining of possessions, such as houses, cars, land, businesses, and commodities of all kinds. These aspects represent signs of wealth and affluence. These are signs of one's 'successful application of power' over reality. The focus is on materiality and the gaining of that power. The messages offered to clarify these points are distorted, however. Power and control are a Djinn concept promoted here to help the children of the fallen to compensate for the feelings of inadequacy and ineffectiveness. This concept is a misdirection of the truth and is not real as is the illusion that one can possess others or material things. The Native Americans were considered savages and uncivilized but possessed the right idea…you rent, or borrow the land from nature, but you cannot possess it. All things gained are on loan for you while you are here. They are like stage props.

The point made is that often possessions or wealth can prevent one from achieving greater awareness because they become a distraction (like something shiny that fascinates but does not gratify). Their relative importance is unimportant, but they could support awareness if held in the correct perspective. This flies in the face of those destitute who are struggling to survive here. Their belief about their deservedness becomes a circular question which, when completed, creates deficit and deprivation. The One wants to suggest cooperation with life, not trying to control it. The One wants to enrich human life through trust in life and in oneself through love and compassion. She wants to introduce the concept that the children are self-responsible for their nightmare. She wants them to know if they change behavior and work cooperatively with the life force, they could alter their nightmare of deficit to greater fulfillment.

She is not responsible for all the terrible things that happen in this dream here. The law of love needed to exist within first, then they could apply the laws from the inside out. To accomplish this, she wanted to appoint someone to be a model here, to become the vessel for these thoughts and feelings of right behavior. This model would lead those willing to change their life and their attitudes. She wanted their lives to reflect her way of inner harmony. She wanted to let them know the outer law imposed by Yahweh to Moses was not her way. Her favored emissary would make this clear.

Centuries before the Christian era, Elijah, a student at the mystery schools of Karnak in Egypt, went to Palestine and rebuilt an old monastery on top of Mount Carmel. There he established his own school of mysteries. When the Essenes first arrived in Palestine, the monastery was supervised by Elijah. After a temporary settlement near Jordan, the Essenes moved on to Galilee near the sea.

The Essenes were Jews by race, but they did not adhere to the Jewish law. Forbidden to the use of animals for sacrifice, they ate vegetarian. Living by their own strict code of conduct, they followed the Mount Carmel White Brotherhood practices of daily meditation and avoiding possessions of wealth. Pooling all their resources together, they paid for their services in the outer community. They often went to those areas outside of the city of Jerusalem where there was sickness and pestilence, healing the sick and taking care of the poor. By the second century B.C., their community grew large, flourishing in several places throughout Palestine. Many Essenes developed skills, such as carpentry, building and weaving, even engaged in construction projects for Rome, but they would not make weapons. All the Jews felt the oppression of the Romans. All had to pledge their allegiance to the Roman emperor and Roman taxation. Often, the regulations would interfere with Jewish religious customs.

Jerusalem was a veritable hotbed of unrest, and for any Roman magistrate ruling over Jerusalem, it was difficult and often felt to be far more of a curse than a blessing. The Jews were very outspoken, often boasting to the Romans that one day a great Jewish king would rule them again as it was in the ancient times. Then, they would no longer have to obey Roman law. This unsettled the Romans. It made them suspicious of any acts which might prove seditious to Roman rule.

Among the Essenes, there were two sects or branches: the Ossaean and the Nazarean. Those of the Nazarean had many in their group who often had visions of someone coming, such as the Ha Mashiach (the Messiah), a would-be savior of the Jewish people. The Nazarenes always spoke of the Ha Mashiach to the poor and downtrodden, giving them hope. The sect functioned near Mount Carmel. Many lived near there. So, after some time, it became known as Nazareth.

The One watched with great interest in these people. She liked what she saw and was happy that they lived modestly, tending to the poor and suffering, and helping the sick. They showed all the qualities of love and compassion she had hoped for in her children, without an outer law forcing them into these behaviors.

She decided these would be the ones to carry the vessel of her word. So, she sent Melchizedek, an angel of the fourth quadrant, near Malandrea. This angel was a changeling. He could become the appearance of any being it met, just by touching.

He descended onto a field of grass on a knoll, near a flock of sheep. Nearby, a shepherd lay against a small clump of rocks. He approached quietly. Without awakening him, he touched him and instantly became the likeness of him. Seeing that the shepherd was wearing a kind of seamless robe, called a garabia, he manifested a similar cloak for himself. He noted the peculiar stripes of color, so he added that just to blend in.

Then the angel entered the village of Nazarenes near Carmel. It was just after dusk. Women assembled around the well in the center of the village, gathering water into goat-skinned sacks slung over their shoulders. They were talking and laughing. They didn't take notice of the stranger amongst them. Melchizedek listened to their words. He hoped to hear them address each other, looking for one specific woman. Her name was Mary.

The women broke up into pairs, a common practice amongst them. Soon, they made their way back to their homes. Two of them bid Mary and her friend farewell. So, he followed them down the pathway toward their hut.

Melchizedek called to Mary. She stopped in her tracks. His voice, unusually deep, sounded melodic. She turned to see the tall stranger standing behind her. Startled because of his unusual size and stature, she saw only his robes covering his head with his face in the shadows. He sensed her fear and spoke.

"Do not be afraid, little one. We mean you no harm."

His tone was soft-spoken and endearing to her. She unconsciously stepped back two paces.

Melchizedek put out his hand, gesturing to hold and quiet her fear.

"Wait! Don't go! He spoke. We've come with a message for you."

The Emissary

Mary's friend grew faint, stumbling right next to her. She grasped her arm to help her over to a small round stone at the side of the path. Her friend was holding her brow and proclaimed.

"Mary! Mary! Why do I feel so dizzy? I'm so tired."

Her friend fell fast asleep right at her feet. This alarmed Mary even more. She spoke in a shaky voice.

"Who are you? And how do you come to know my name?"

The angel paused for a moment before he spoke again.

"We are but a shepherd, come to tend to the Most high's flock. We have good news for you, Mary. They have rewarded your prayers and visions. The One greets you with love and compassion. She sends blessings and wishes you to flourish. She has anointed you Mary to be the one who will bear a son. He shall be the vessel of the Ha Mashiach, the Christ consciousness."

Mary was even more frightened than before.

"But I am a vestal virgin. I cannot bear children. They forbid it! I'm without a spouse, so how can this be?"

Melchizedek continued.

"Do not fret or worry, Mary. For the One is with you always. She has made it possible for you to be with spouse. Even now unto this moment, one of your brethren will come. At the first crow of the cock, he will come to you. He will propose to you for your hand in marriage. All will know it foreordained this by the One in heaven. She hopes that this is so. She has called you and now you must choose."

Mary turned for a moment to glance at her friend, still lying asleep. Then, she turned back again to look at the stranger, but he vanished, without a sound. She looked around but could not find where he had gone. Without further thought on this strange incident, she knelt to tend to her friend, who was just awakening. In the first light of the next day, at the crow of the cock, Joseph appeared at Mary's hut and asked to be received. He wasted no time to tell her of a strange dream he experienced the night before. Also, he proclaimed the need to propose to her to be his wife. Tears rolled down her face. She proclaimed her visit with a stranger, an angel she concluded, on that same eve. He had told her that this would happen.

Together, they came before the council of the brotherhood of Nazarenes. There was much argument and disbelief. They proclaimed her virginity. The Mosaic law was simple; vestal virgins shall remain so until they're passing.

"Elijah himself wrote it." They spoke.

Joseph pleaded with the leaders. "Brothers, don't you see?" This is the moment we have hoped and waited so long for. Why are you so resistant to abide by the Lord's will?" One leader stood up. His name was Cephus.

"Dear brother Joseph. We appreciate your zeal, and we can appreciate your desire to have a wife, to bear your children. But the law states, it is forbidden to marry a virgin. We will find another wife for you. There are plenty of matchmakers in the community, Joseph. You know the law!"

At that moment, Joseph looked at Mary and she him. She burst into tears, sobbing at his chest. Then just before the council disbanded, there was a great flash of light within the makeshift temple anteroom. Women were not allowed in the synagogue. Standing before them, were three angels. One of them was Melchizedek.

"Why do you rebuke the word of your Lord? Your brother and sister have come before you are speaking the truth. You ask your mother in heaven for her help and this is how you repay her, with your petty quarrels, doubts, and disobedience! Perhaps it would be wise to return to tell the One you are unworthy of her grace!"

The council and everyone else in the room were prostrate at the feet of these amazing creatures standing before them. Their faces buried in the dust and not daring to look upon their countenance. Cephus, with outstretched hand called out.

"Please forgive us our ignorance. How could we know your divine will?"

Melchizedek smiled at Cephus.

"Get up!" Do not bow before us! We are not your God, but only her messengers come to proclaim the glory of the Nameless One and her unconditional love. Though I do not see what she sees in you pathetic creatures! Yet, it is her divine will that it be so. May the One Most High find mercy upon you and grant you clemency."

With that they vanished. The room was silent except for some weeping amongst the women near the door. Cephus broke the silence by proclaiming a wedding celebration, with all the community attending. Later, trouble was soon to follow. On the night of their nuptials and the first conjugal visit, Mary conceived their child on that same night. It was not long after, she showed. Joseph went to the rabbi of the community and complained that Mary may have already defiled her virginity before he knew her. He claimed with anger, she wanted his name to cover the multitudes of her sin, for she must have been with child before their marriage. After hearing his petitions, they agreed that Mary was to suffer without fellowship of the community for five months, while they deliberated on the issue. Joseph wanted the marriage annulled, but the rabbi was not so keen to break apart what the angels put together.

A new wrinkle surfaced. King Herod became aware of the Ha Mashiach prophecies. He also knew his right to rule would be questioned and usurped by the Ha Mashiach. He had to eliminate the threat. So, he went to the Roman Magistrate. He made his petition that they should kill all first born, two years old or less.

The angel Melchizedek once again came to Earth and appeared to Joseph in the middle of the night. He explained Mary had been chaste the whole time before their marriage. The One wanted the child to manifest without delay.

"Joseph! Awaken Joseph!"

Joseph sat up, startled. "Who's there?" He said with a shaking voice.

Then the angel appeared before him. Joseph dropped to his knees and prostrated himself before the angel's brilliant light. "Be not afraid! It is the Lord that calls upon you Joseph. Do not be angry with Mary, for she has been chaste. We came to warn you that Mary is in grave danger. The soldiers are coming to bring harm. You must go now and take her away from this place tonight."

Then Melchizedek vanished. Joseph wasted no time to gather his belongings, such as they were, and rushed to Mary's hut. He told her what had happened. They left, telling no one. While on the journey to Egypt, he expressed his regret for doubting her. He vouched for her safety with his life. They bore the child Jeshua in the middle of the night in a quiet countryside in a shepherd's hut near the road between Egypt and Palestine. They were alone except for a few sheep and their donkey.

Three magi, traveling on the road to Egypt from the East, stopped to rest near to them. They shared food and drink and explained to Joseph and Mary that they were on a quest to follow a passing of a comet. The Magi believed the comet to be a sign, fulfilling a prophecy of an influential leader coming, foretold long ago by the stars. They were not even aware that Joseph, Mary, and Jeshua were the ones they were looking for! In the early morning they left, bidding each a pleasant journey. Nine years passed. Mary birthed two other children while in Egypt. The other births weakened her health. Joseph could not care for her and their children alone, so they returned to Carmel seeking the support of their spiritual family. Jeshua seemed fearless as a young boy. Often, he would wonder off into the desert and not return for days. Then later, Jeshua returned exhausted from the heat and delirious from dehydration. Joseph found the boy often willful and somewhat disobedient. But when Jeshua suffered strange and debilitating fits from time to time, Joseph's heart would soften. Though healers tended to him often, no one in the community seemed to help ease his malady. When Jeshua turned twelve, Joseph brought him to Jerusalem while he negotiated the exchange of goods in the marketplace. He brought Jeshua to show him the city and to teach him the art of negotiation. While Joseph became engrossed in the heat of a bargain, Jeshua disappeared into the crowd. Joseph became alarmed because slave traders always looked for stray young boys. He broke off the bargaining, now angry at looking for him. After looking for him for hours, he noticed men heading to the Great Synagogue. He asked them if they had seen a young boy passing. "Excuse me, sir. Have you seen a young boy passing nearby? He was wearing a light blue garabia and a tunic too large for him."

The men laughed.

"You have just described half of the beggars in Jerusalem! We've learned today, there is a new rabbi speaking at the temple. Why don't you join us? Perhaps prayers will help you find him."

Joseph sat against a small ledge along the wall of the temple. He lamented to himself bringing Jeshua to the city was a mistake. Then he felt a strange urge to go in with the other men. When they entered the great hall, Joseph heard a familiar voice. It was Jeshua! To his amazement, he found him speaking to hundreds of people gathered around him. Even more amazing, he was quoting scripture by heart, by book and verse as any rabbi could.

Joseph never taught him any of the scripture. Jeshua was too young to make the Bar Mitzvah rites. Joseph stood in the hypostyle, looking on in astonishment, wondering when he would retrieve his son. He was concerned that he was making a fool of them. Then he noticed it. Just behind and above Jeshua, a soft golden light emanated and illuminated only him. Jeshua's appearance showed a countenance about his face. Though his urge was to stop this, he held back. Later, upon their return to Carmel, Joseph went to the elders and explained to them what happened in Jerusalem. They concluded it was time that young Jeshua, begin his training. Jeshua entered the monastery at Mount Carmel, where he studied the secret mysteries of the temple Karnack for three years. On the conclusion of his training there, at fifteen years of age, he left Galilee to study in Nepal. He would spend five more years in India developing his mind and training his will with the Rishis. Then he left Nepal to enter the Himalayas of Tibet and continued for another ten years to learn Donpo, a healing art and the pohah, an out-of-body projection practice. Then, he returned to Persia to study with the Sung Moon brotherhood, learning the ancient practice of energy transformation and spiritual alkemi. Later, he returned to Palestine at 30, ready to begin his ministry. He sat one evening, in the garden of Gethsemane, in meditation under the light of a full moon. An angel appeared to him. It was the archangel, Michael. "Blessings upon you, Jeshua. The One is pleased with you and finds you worthy to receive her anointing."

Jeshua knelt upon his knees, lifting his head with tears streaming from his eyes. "I am ready, Mother." At that moment, Michael placed his hand on Jeshua's head. A glorious light poured down upon him. His body shook. He fell to the ground, folded into a fetal position. A great seizure, like his childhood experiences, came over him. Inside, he could hear a low voice speaking to him. "And lo, my son, though we are with you always, you will be our words, our mind, our heart to my children. You are now the Ha Mashiach, the vessel of Our Holy Spirit, the Christ Force. This will be so for three years. During these three years, you will teach and heal the sick and cast out daemons. Teach my children well. In this time gather unto yourself those for whom you deem fit, those who you can trust to extend Our words that We will give you. Known for you in the Earth, all things humans are divided. And so, you shall have one to assist you in handling those other female aspects. You will know her through her flaming hair. She will be with an indignant attitude toward all men.

You will take this one for your wife, though it will be strange for a rabbi to do this. It will be those near you who will carry the Keys of Light, which will open the gates of our kingdom to all humankind forever." The light and the angel Michael vanished. Jeshua wept while still lying on the cold ground, shaking from head to toe. He mumbled to himself under the stars. By the light of the next day, he became a fisher of men. It would not be long before he would gather unto himself the inner circle of twelve disciples, then after the next circle of twenty-four disciples and then finally the outer circle of thirty-six disciples, making seventy-two in all. When he entered Antioch, there he found a woman of substantial wealth and influence. She was outspoken about the injustices of men regarding women. The fire of Sukon burned radiantly along her curls of bright red hair. He knew then he had found her, Mary the Magdalene. Jeshua immediately took Mary and him by her. She became his confidant and closest friend. She would advise him on the most important affairs. Though he was a true visionary, she saw he was also unorganized. In her bold manner, she was confident about taking charge over practical matters. Mary helped him plan his strategy of outreach to other communities. Simon, later known as Peter, opposed her attitude right from the start. He opposed her managing the Master in her own way. He perceived her to be arrogant, to a fault. Timothy was the first to complain to Jeshua about her. "Master. Why is she with us? You are always with her these days. It is difficult for us, me, to have fellowship with you anymore!"

Jeshua stared at him before he spoke.

"Timothy, you are saying much, but little about the truth in your heart. Speak your heart, brother." Timothy paused, as if to prepare for a greater confrontation.

"Well master. Frankly, you seemed to love Mary more than us now!"

John and James agreed. Then the others chimed in. Then Simon stepped forward. "Master. Why do we need her? We were doing okay before she came!"

Jeshua responded sharply.

"Simon, I'm surprised at you… you over all the others. Are you a part of this too? Our ability to reach out has been more effective now with her help. She has helped to clothe us, helped to feed us on our journeys and often bribes the Centurions when we need to enter restricted areas. Though I know you do not want to accept that, it is true. I need her. She needs me, and she is invaluable. I plan we should wed at the earliest opportunity."

Bartholomew challenged Jeshua.

"Master! You can't be serious! I'm sorry, but you're a rabbi. How would it look? It's bad enough you spend so much of your time drinking with tax collectors and harlots. People are talking. We must explain your actions. We must make excuses for the 'evil' rabbi."

Jeshua raised his hand to them while he looked at Bartholomew.

"So, you would make excuses for your Master, and for the One in heaven as well? Who are you, in this? Do the sheep now make excuses for the shepherd?"

Bartholomew bowed his head with shame as Jeshua continued.

"My love for all of you is far greater than you can comprehend. You are all my brothers now. I expect you to search your hearts, find the wisdom not to judge her, or me. Be careful, lest you be judged in your last days here. She stays, and that is final. Deal with your feelings, as need be on this. I will hear no more of it!"

Thomas chimed in.

"Well, I like her! And I'm glad she is with us."

James turned to him and laughed.

"Yes, that's because she does your laundry, and we all know you dream about her at night!"

At that remark, Thomas punched James in the stomach. Then they all laughed, including Jeshua. The tasks and burden of Jeshua's ministry grew larger as more learned of Jeshua's teachings about the love and compassion for their fellow brethren. Soon, he could not tend to all that requested his presence. So, he began out-of-body projections to handle the masses in so many places. The effort was exhausting. When he returned, Mary would tend to him, bathing his tired feet with herbs and fine oils from Egypt and Persia, while also massaging his weary body.

Jeshua was news. The word of his exploits spread to the Sanhedrin and Rome. Word of their concern from Rome returned to Pontius Pilate...this prophet was gathering the people together. Rome worried Jeshua would excite the Jews for an insurrection in Jerusalem. Centurians were spread thin on other fronts. They did not want to send more troops to the city to keep the peace. So, they appealed to Pontius Pilate to go to Caiaphas, head of the Sanhedrin, to speak of the young rabbi.

The sounds of discussion rang loud in the halls of the Great Synagogue of Jerusalem. Much of the discussion and argument surrounded Jeshua's exploits and his ability to perform miracles. He preached of a New Kingdom. Jeshua entered the synagogue with James and John on either side of him. Caiaphas raised his hand to bring order to the body of Pharisees and Sadducees. Caiaphas spoke first.

"Welcome young rabbi. We've heard much about your ministry and admire your zeal for the scriptures. Nicodemus here seems to think you bring a new life to the holy words, unlike any prophet before. We are more interested in your prophecies about a New Kingdom. Many are saying you are the self-proclaimed king of that Kingdom. What do you say to this?"

Jeshua looked at Nicodemus and smiled before he spoke.

"It is the Kingdom of my mother in heaven I speak of."

Caiaphas reacted to these words.

"You dare to speak of our God as female and in the same vein as yourself? This is blasphemous!"

Jeshua responded.

"Do you not know already that she is Mother to all?"

Caiaphas continued to challenge him.

"What say you to your declaration that the laws of Moses are dead to the world, that a new law, your law, replaces the old law? Your call for love between brethren is commendable, but to rebuke the laws of our forefathers that were handed down to us from our God on Sinai is dangerous! Perhaps it is even seditious, young rabbi. With these words you bring chaos and a disruption to our society, and trouble from the Rome as well. Are you not breaking the laws of Moses?"

Jeshua lowered his head, shaking it from side to side. He

began still looking down at the floor.

"Great and honorable Caiaphas, try to understand. We do not come to break your law, but to fulfill it. Our Kingdom is not of this world. Is it not written that one would come to bring life to that which is dead to the spirit? Do you not know, the god of your fathers is a false god and had misled Moses?"

Caiaphas again spoke in anger.

"Again, young rabbi, you speak blasphemous words. Are you claiming to be the Ha Mashiach?"

Jeshua remained silent. Caiaphas then charged him again.

"I am High Priest of the Sanhedrin. I honor the law before the one true God that leads this body of priests with chaste and with purity of heart, unchallenged. Yet, you make these claims while you cavort with fornicators, harlots, and tax collectors. You imbibe the fruit of the vine. Are these the acts of a true Ha Mashiach, or at the least, a rabbi?"

Jeshua answered strongly to this challenge.

"You are as vipers hiding behind a holy station. You speak of the law, but your hearts are venomous with judgment, arrogant with power. Your hearts are as dead as stone. You know the truth of what we speak, but you do not bring this truth to those who need it. We find greater openness to the truth amongst those less fortunate, those burdened with tasks most would not want to do. We find the light shines best where there is darkness, but with some humbleness. Those for whom you speak are more honorable than you! Yes. They are not chaste and commit sins against their brothers and sisters, but they are honest with these deeds. They are ignorant of the truth and do not put on airs about what they are. It is with these we feel welcomed. It will be these that I can teach, for their cups are empty while yours is full!"

Caiaphas turned to the other Pharisees and Sadducees.

"Well, brothers, you have heard for yourself these things from this so-called 'prophet of the poor, the sinners and overburdened.' We have here is another false prophet before us, not the Ha Mashiach. Leave us now, evil rabbi. Do not defile our faith with your blasphemy any further!" Jeshua, James, and John left without further comment. Joseph of Arimathea and Nicodemus approached Caiaphas after.

"Eminence, why did you chastise him so? You, of all people, know of the value of his testimony, even the possibility he may in fact be the one we have been hoping for... the Ha Mashiach."

Caiaphas spoke.

"Brothers, you do not understand the precarious political nature of the situation. Our role here is tenuous. We must be politicians and priests. There is much to balance here. We stand between the unbelievers, those whose faith is waning on the one hand, while the Romans make our lives more difficult with every passing day. It would be with little provocation that they close our temple next, blocking the rest of our opportunities to worship. We must be cautious in our actions. Are we disciples of this young one, no? But he understands the nature of our situation. Besides, I have a plan to bring the Romans into the fold. Then, perhaps, all will be well again."

It was near the end of Jeshua's third year of the Christ

The Emissary

infusion from the One. Jeshua had even made Pontius Pilate a disciple. Caiaphas' plan to bring harmony between the Romans and the Sanhedrin was now undermined. Rome's emperor, Julius Caesar, died, leaving the new emperor, Tiberius, deciding to make an example of Jerusalem. He reinstated and enforced new rules and regulations, increasing the taxes of all Roman territories. His edict that all acts of sedition would be punishable by death placed the Sanhedrin in a difficult position.

The zealots misunderstood Jeshua's teachings. They believed his Kingdom would be the reinstatement of the Jewish Nation. He would reign over their Kingdom with his might and power, freeing them of Roman rule and taxation. They began an outcry of rebellion against the Romans, making Jeshua's proclamation of a New Kingdom synonymous with their new Jewish Nation. They made him the spearhead of their movement. It was not long before orders from the emperor himself came to the office of Pontius Pilate... hunt down this prophet of sedition. Make an example of him for all to see. Caiaphas sent word to Jeshua through known contacts close to him. He was in the hills near the Mount of Olives when he got word of the worsening situation in Rome. There was a price on his head. Caiaphas warned him not to make any public appearances. Jeshua did not fear these reports because he could be out of the body in many places at once, making it almost impossible for them to catch him. He grew concerned for Mary. She had secretly wed with him in Copernicum and already bearing him two children. His family was his greatest weakness, as he could no longer guarantee their safety. He met with Joseph of Arimathea in the catacombs under the city of Jerusalem. It was a secret place for the disciples to meet. There, Joseph told him of his concern. Jeshua expressed his concern.

"Brother Joseph, you know of the danger. I'm concerned for Mary and the children. If anything should happen, I want you to take them to Balthazar, in Persia. He will have the means to protect them." Joseph responded with a hug and a kiss on the cheek.

"Yes, as you wish, master."

Days later, Jeshua prepared a small feast for his inner circle. There he began a sacred ceremony in which he imparted the bread and wine with the spirit of the Christ energy in which he shared with his closest disciples.

"Eat and drink, brothers, for you devour your master tonight, both in body and in blood. Time is short and things will change. You will carry the Keys of your Mother's Kingdom to the rest of the world. Listen to Simon, whom I will now call Peter. Even though, with the sound of the third crow of the cock, he shall deny me, he will still be the example of strength that will bind you together. He will be the outer rock upon which the temple inside you shall flourish."

John spoke together with Thomas.

"Master, you speak as though you are leaving."

Thomas added.

"Where are you going?"

Jeshua spoke again.

The Emissary

"Lo, this will be the last meal we share. I will soon pass from your midst and there will be rumors of this passing, but do not be alarmed. I will always be with you." They ate the rest of the meal in silence. All felt the heaviness of their master's heart. Then Jeshua moved closer to Judas, confiding in him so that the others could not hear his words. He had a terrible burden to give him. "Judas, I know you love me more than most." Judas' tears filled his eyes. It is because of your love for me, I will ask a great favor of you."

Judas sobbed more.

"Anything for you, master… anything."

Jeshua poured more wine into his cup.

"I will need you to betray me to the Romans tonight!"

Judas wept and dropped his head on the table, pulling at his hair. The others looked up at him and wondered why he was crying. Judas pleaded with Jeshua.

"Please master, anything but that. How could I do such a terrible thing? I love you with all my heart."

Jeshua continued.

"I know that Judas. It is because of your great loving heart; they choose you to be the only one I can trust to do this. It is a terrible burden I place upon you because your brothers will come to despise you and hate you for my sake."

Judas looked at him in bewilderment.

"But why master?"

Jeshua placed his hand on Judas' head and smiled.

"My friend, it is because you are strong. You can do it! You can find me in the garden. They will make the way to my location known you"

Judas continued to weep. He drank more wine until he was drunk with it. He now looked at Jeshua with some anger in his eyes. Judas got up from the table and stumbled out of the catacombs, heading for the Roman magistrate's office in the Roman Garrison above. Later that night, Jeshua sought refuge in the garden of Gethsemane, a place where he found solace in his meditations. It was late. Most disciples huddled together to rest against the cold of the night. The angel Michael came to him again.

"Jeshua, your mother is pleased with your work, but the time of the Christ Force joining is over."

At that moment, Michael placed his hand on his head, and the light left him. He dropped to the ground, shaking with another seizure. He was alone and naked in the night. The warmth and strength of the One was gone. Once again, he was a simple man. He could hear a voice speaking in a whisper to him. The angel Michael spoke for the One.

"Dear sweet Jeshua, your monumental task is almost over now. But the time ahead will be difficult for you. Your life will remain a thankless task, but we will always be with you. So, do not despair. They will torture you and rebuke you for our sake."

He lay there, still shaking. Tears rolled down his face as he pleaded.

"Mother, I am afraid. Please pass this cup from me."

There was no response. Jeshua spoke again and then reminded of the One's silence, of his commitment to the light worlds.

"It is not of my will, but it is your will that I shall abide."

Then his somber moment got disturbed by the sound of soldiers clumping through the garden. They had come for him. He realized, to his chagrin, his friend Judas found the strength to carry out his wish.

Meanwhile, Pontius Pilate, together with Caiaphas, laid out a clever plan to get Jeshua out of harm's way by faking his death through his crucifixion. This plan, known only to a few... Simon Peter, Pontius Pilate, Jeshua, and Caiaphas. Not even Mary and the other disciples knew of the plan. They would administer a drug used in the Essene Brotherhood for suspended animation practice before they put him onto the tree. While on his way to the place of crucifixion, he would fall under the weight of carrying the tree twice. His brother would carry the tree the rest of the way not to the mound of Golgotha, but to a place on Joseph of Arimathea's property, in view of Golgotha. While he was apart from the procession, they would give him the drug. The suppression of his life signs would not take effect until catalyzed by vinegar.

[Note to the reader:] It was customary to break the legs of anyone who got crucified to quicken their death through suffocation. In Jeshua's case, orders were not to break Jeshua's legs, but to let him die, by course. This was to save his life. That afternoon, they nailed his wrists with both arms stretched above and together. They nailed together also his feet with his legs crossed and placed upon a small step mounted to the long pole, already cleaned of bark.

[Note to the reader:] There was no cross member, as is so often depicted in the artwork of the Middle Ages. We believe the source of this inspiration to be pagan. The Romans were efficient and did not waste lumber on crucifixions. When he proclaimed his thirst and asked for water, it was a sign that he was ready. Simon stepped forward and offered him vinegar to drink. This put him into the expected suspended state and within five hours, the Roman soldiers declared him dead. After being declared dead, he was removed into the hands of the Initiates and taken to Joseph's family tomb for burial.

Mary left the children with Salome, her other sister, while she stayed and witnessed his crucifixion and death. When he collapsed and the soldiers pronounced him dead, she couldn't believe it. She screamed and broke down into tears. She and her sister Martha left still sobbing before the disciples took him down from the pole, wrapped his body in white raiment, and took him to Joseph's tomb. The drug took almost two days to wear off.

In the meantime, his mother, Mary the Magdalene, and her sisters brought oils to anoint his body before they rolled the stone to cover the tomb. For the next few days, the disciples stayed in Joseph's house, still in shock, and tried to console themselves with their desperate feelings of loss and abandonment. Mary went to Simon Peter, asking to go where he laid to rest. She gathered her sisters and Jeshua's mother to the tomb. Mary demanded that the tomb be uncovered, and the soldiers complied. Mary found the place where he lay empty, with only the raiment draped over the slab. She queried the soldiers to find out if anyone had been there before, but they denied anyone had come. Mary concluded Jeshua had ascended. She spread the word amongst the disciples. They had a difficult time to believe her story since it would be her to discover it. Mathew complained.

"Why do you come here to torture us with this news? Can you not, see? Our Master is dead, and we are dealing with his loss! Leave us be, woman!"

Thomas always expressed doubt about everything. Even he snapped at her.

"I won't... I can't believe it! Not until I can stick my fingers into his wounds, will I believe our Master has risen!"

Mary yelled in frustration at them all.

"Do you think this is what he would have wanted? To just sit around and feel sorry for yourselves! You think I would tell you such a thing just to get attention? Well, if you think that, then you are all stupid and deserve to suffer!"

She stormed out. Mary was never to see many of them again after that. The situation became worse in Jerusalem. Zealots made random attacks against the Romans everywhere. All the disciples were fragmented and couldn't agree on anything. Everyone held onto their own ideas about how things happened. The disciples were illiterate men. They could not record their experiences. Simon Peter could not keep them together. They were all talking about returning to their ordinary lives. So, he took their minds off their troubles by sending them out to teach, two by two.

Simon Peter came to Mary, telling her it wasn't safe. He

explained about her husband's wish that she goes to Balthazar in Persia along with the children until it was safe to send for her. It wasn't long after her arrival in Persia that zealots tracked her whereabouts. She and the children then had to leave again.

Simon Peter was called to Rome on urgent matters. So, he sent Joseph of Arimathea, James, and John to escort Mary and the children to France. Martha, her sister, also joined them. Later, they arrived safely in Baume.

Meanwhile, Simon Peter arrived in Rome to find that the emperor Tiberius had died. Caligula already assumed the throne, proclaiming himself as Caesar. He summoned Simon Peter to the palace. The premise was that he wanted to talk about the future of the Christians. Several Praetorian guards greeted Simon Peter at the palace steps, making him feel more like a prisoner than a guest. They took him before Caesar in the main throne room. There he found Pontius Pilate standing near Caligula on his right. Peter nodded to acknowledge Pilate. Pilate nodded back to him in return. Caligula spoke first in a condescending tone.

"So, you are the one they call Peter the leader of the rebellion in Jerusalem?"

Peter paused before answering.

"Yes Caesar. I am called Simon by some and more recently, Peter by others."

He did not acknowledge the challenge that he was a rebel leader.

He continued.

"The ones you refer to are zealots seeking to undermine your Roman rule. We do not seek to advocate such violence. We are about teaching others from the words of our master to love one another."

Caligula continued to probe.

"Does that love include the devotion to a king that challenges my absolute rule of Rome?"

There was a pause for an answer, but he didn't wait and went on.

"My sources tell me that there is another. One who was more connected to your dead Messiah King, the one they call Mary. You know about this one, yes? You traveled with them while they were together? We understand they were married in Copernicum.... You know of this too... yes?"

Peter dropped his head down before answering.

"Yes, great Caesar. We know of her."

Caesar added.

"This woman is trouble for us. We strongly feel she and her children are a threat to Rome! So, we place before you a choice. Reveal to us the precise whereabouts of these vile creatures of the madman called Jeshua, and we will reward you with your life and the lives of your other friends. If not, then you will die by crucifixion along with all your friends today! Oh, and please realize that if we spare your lives, this reprieve does not mean we will sanction your continued preaching of this peculiar sedition called Christianity."

Simon Peter had no great allegiance toward Mary and her outspoken ways. Her behavior, as far as he was concerned, was unforgivable. If it was to be a matter of choice to save her or saving his beloved friends, his brother's disciples, it was no contest. He made no secret of his feelings toward Mary frequently with the master, regarding her role in the master's mission here. She wanted to usurp the key role in his master's life and punish him. After all, she was only a woman! There was no way he would allow such an opportunity to preserve the teachings among his brethren to slip by on her behalf. Peter felt sure that her demise would mean little now since the master had left them. He gave no thought regarding the children. He assumed Caligula would place them in one of the salt mines in Thrace to wither and die on the chains of Roman slavery. But he misjudged the capacity of this cruel Caesar to rule without a second thought. So, with grim determination and with complete justification to the cause, Simon Peter revealed her location to Caligula.

"I have myself arranged for her and the children to be taken to France. It is a place called Baume. You will find her there!" Caligula smiled like a Cheshire cat with delight.

"Peter...Simon, or whatever your name is, you are free to go! Remember, you are not to spread anymore of this Christianity, or you will feel the sting of the tree! Now leave us! We'll have no more of your kind to spoil our day!"

Simon Peter left the palace mumbling. The deal with Caligula went through his mind over and over arguing his questionable actions. He knew he had put his master's wife and his children to death. He reasoned that since the master was gone, he was the only one left to make sure the Christian movement would survive the whims and onslaughts of this new Caesar's hatred. Many Christians had died for less. So, why not let her sacrifice something for the cause? One day in Baume, while Mary shopped in the village, Martha and three men near the cave where they stayed confronted the children. The first man stopped her and spoke.

"Are you the one they call Mary?"

Martha became alarmed for her sister's life and responded. "Yes."

At that point, they pulled swords from their garabias and plunged them into her heart. As she lay dying, the children fell upon her, crying. Then, without hesitation, the men killed both children. They looked around to check for any reactions in their surroundings, then fled. Upon Mary's return, she found them lying on the ground drenched in blood surrounded by a small crowd. She fell upon their bodies, devastated. She screamed in bitter sadness at her loss of Jeshua. Now her children and beloved sister were also gone. She became angry with the Highest and cried out to her.

"Why do you demand so much of me? Wasn't it enough that you took Jeshua from me? Now you have taken my only remnant, my children, and even my sister in my place! Lord, Mother in heaven, have you no mercy? What have I done to deserve this?"

The One did not answer her. Mary spent many months in silence inside the cave. She would not eat or care for herself while she mourned her loss. Many in the village took care of her needs until she recovered. Meanwhile, Jeshua went to

Egypt, where he stayed hidden within the tombs just outside Cairo. His bargain with Pontius Pilate, upon his disappearance and apparent crucifixion, the disciples would not be harmed, nor would Mary and the children be harmed. He visited Mary in Sainte Baume, out of body, just before the zealots had come.

She assumed he had died and ascended. She was very sad. It never occurred to her he was still alive. Jeshua was happy that she was safe with the children. He had made several visitations to the disciples, also out of body, continuing to teach them about the mysteries for several more years. He died at seventy-three of consumption. Jeshua remained secretly buried within the tombs of Egypt, where he ascended upon his death.

Years passed. Caligula blamed the plight of Rome on the scourge of the Christians. He wished to put an end to the Christian blight upon Rome and began an all-out campaign to wipe them out. That included those remaining disciples that were hunted down and crucified one by one. Mary the Magdalen remained in Sainte Baume, serving the local community through her healing efforts for the rest of her life.

She began the Priory of Zion, a close-knit group of artisans, scribes, and noblemen with whom she shared her knowledge. She remained the only living bearer of the knowledge of the Keys of the Kingdom, which she passed onto the Knights of Christ(the Cathars) and then finally to the Knights Templar, a group of spiritual knights sworn to protect the Keys until the world was ready to receive them. Mary's identity remained secret. I knew her only as the 'Holy Grail,' the divine cup of grace.

Other Heavens, Other Earths

There is a reference in a biblical passage from the Book of John, Chapter Fourteen. It says, "In my father's house there are many mansions, if it were not so, I would have told you." Like so many other passages in the Bible, it is a stand-alone passage that remains obscure and indefinable, at least from the normal religious perspective.

In the overall sense, the One's story defined her realm and the Earth regarding the fallen. The Earth is both a true manifestation in the astral sense but also it is metaphorical in the sense there are many Earths in other parts of her realm. But we also consider that within her realm there are many Earths as there are probabilities along an infinite number of timelines. Those Earths have the same number of heavens.

To consider other universes living alongside ours is a startling thought. Though this idea is often revealed through several science fiction movies and television shows, it has its roots in several scientific theories, including some mathematical papers written by Albert Einstein. One might consider this as impossible, but if you wait 'five years', one might find the possibility looming into view. Things change sometimes drastically. As Shakespeare once wrote, 'there are more things in heaven and earth than are dreamt of in your philosophy.'

Not that long-ago people could hardly understand there were other cultures experiencing life in other places on earth as passionately and as tragically as anyone else. They make this reality possible because of the worldwide proliferation of news provided by satellite transmissions, global computer networks and transcontinental communications. These realities were not possible even a hundred years ago. So, the world became smaller for everyone. The focus had been in one's own backyard and now the focus is upon the backyards of everyone else, so to speak.

In the same way, people think the universe revolves around the Earth with all its trials, tribulations, and elations. Even though Galileo invented the telescope to prove otherwise, the church kept the focus here and not out there. Yet, all that would come to a grinding halt the minute that extraterrestrials take flight and land here wanting to contact everyone. That may sound like science fiction to most non-believers, but everyday scientists are changing their ideas about life on other planets. According to the most recent reports, they have found far more planets than stars in the universe, with many more chances that life exists beyond the Earth. The possibility of contact looms larger with every day that passes.

This idea brings mixed reactions. On the one hand, it would be comforting to know there is other life out there with so much space to contend with. It is depressing to realize that we are not the only darlings of God's creation. It must feel like the only child enjoying the full attention of the parents and then to discover it has one or more siblings in which it now must share that attention.

Another common point made is that man has been made in God's 'image'. This might suggest a genetic image, perhaps.

Many people think God has two arms, two legs and wears a long white beard together with flowing robes as depicted in Michelangelo's painting in the Cysteine Chapel. This is, to sensitive feelings, not accurate. There is a spiritual correspondence the body takes regarding its shape as it relates to the spiritual composition of the imprint. There is also the genetic make-up of the human as an animal. It is a mix, like it or not. The church has trained us to ignore our animal heritage in deference to the spiritual heritage. Like so many other aspects here, it polarizes everything, especially the state of the human as a spirit versus the animal.

The image of God reflecting in man is his 'soul'. This idea came from the Anunnaki father god Jehovah, or Yahweh. The spiritual doctrine of the 'soul' begins there in the garden of Edan. The exact composition of the 'soul' and even its reality is obscure from the church's teachings to the masses, except that the church declares the 'soul' is flawed (tainted by sin) and needs to be saved. But they also say the 'soul 'is eternal? If it is eternal, why does it have to be saved? The so called 'soul' is really a collection of experiences from imprints gathered over many cycles of life that offer a separate perspective and immolate self-consciousness.

So, what does this mean about other life in the universe? Is it then justified that any other life other than human life is not of 'god's kingdom? (But which 'god' are we talking about?) From the point of view of the original religious idea, it would seem logical they would have to be the 'children of Cain', outcasts from paradise. Scientists have predicted other life may not look like human meaning; one head, two arms, two legs, and walking upright while speaking our language. Using the Galapagos Islands as an example of natural evolution, we conclude that life would develop according to the circumstances and environment of the immediate surroundings.

The situation on this Earth is unique from other Earths. The fallen have degenerated with experiences they have imbued into and represent the animal bodies here. That is not the case everywhere else in the universe. Animals can develop into higher life forms as primates, for example, rising to greater intelligence and flourishing as civilizations with greater technology than our own. They do not possess 'souls' because there is no reincarnation process elsewhere. They are from and represent life in all its variations. In this alone, we need to and must respect all life in its infinite variations. There is no reason to think life under non-fallen influences would be any better or any less in value than life under the fallen experience. Perhaps under the unfallen, in some of the lower realms, they may have achieved a higher standard of moral values such as, no war, no disease and a high social development. Then we need to tip our spiritual hat and take note. If the fallen could recover what they lost, then they would have something more within their experience than those who have not fallen. The experience of a reduction in consciousness will stand as a worthwhile but unfortunate experience in and by itself. It would also define a greater resolve about love and compassion in the unity of consciousness. Their strength would be the pillars upon which the One would create a greater, stronger realm that beholds her light for all to experience. Those that have recovered will be co-creators like no other. They will exceed the One's original intent. She is pleased about that prospect. It is one of the outstanding qualities about the One that goes well beyond the other Djinn. Her willingness to allow something greater than herself to flourish comes from it not diminishing her light. In fact, it increases her light. This is because she is the first of her kind. She will always be ahead of any recent development because she will always be first. Any recent development can expand to the fullest no matter how great the evolution and that will always be in her dust.

Her unconditional love and compassion stand above all the Djinn as the most viable approach to reality, with complete trust in free will and without the rigid control and fear proposed by the Djinn.

Yet, we must also consider the One from an alien point of view. She does not come from around here and does not fit in with any of our present moral codes. Hers are a higher standard one should think! Yet, it's unfortunate that people become very uncomfortable with higher energy vibrations and snarl and bite. One cannot accept her presence without accepting one's own being. This whole idea that one is not worthy of being in her presence is ridiculous. To feel shy or to feel ashamed to be in her presence of unconditional love, understanding, and compassion is nothing short of pride. The One's only request is that one would wish to be with her more than anything one values, including oneself. If one would go the whole nine yards to greet her, she would pave the way right to one's doorstep. One might ponder why she doesn't come here often? She is not ashamed of humans! It is because our vibrations are so stiff and slow; it is difficult for her to be here. The vibrations here are painful to light world beings. So, she often sends angels to offer support and wisdom to humans. The shame and unworthiness are hard for her to take. We have the church to thank for that.

We expect one to bring oneself to the altar, but then the priesthood intervenes to interpret because they are more holy than thou! History has shown us that the priesthood has not been a shining example for us to follow. All that is required to communicate is an open mind and a pure heart. Churches burden the children of the fallen with fear, shame, and guilt. It is the imprint's responsibility to clear away that garbage if it can. The imprint needs to forgive itself for its shortcomings. Then it needs to move on to higher ground. All the Gnostic gospels say, 'there is no necessity for an intermediary between the One and the devotee.' The priesthood has been very busy trying to keep everyone from discovering that fact.

The perspective has been from heaven. Now, it is time to look at heaven from the human perspective. In the ancient, alchemical expression given by the famed Hermes Trismegistus; as above, so below, there is a direct corollary, between what is going on in heaven and what is going on in the Earth.

For the children of the fallen as human beings, experience life on the Earth as a separate physical experience. They recognize nothing as spiritual beyond those physical forces that are obvious and beyond human control, such as storms, earthquakes, volcanoes or any other atmospheric or planetary influences, which may wreak havoc in their lives. Other than that, we have only the Christian remnants of the gospels, along with biblical history offered by the church, or other spiritual traditions from Asia or the Middle East. What if these remnants are incomplete? Worse, what if they misinterpreted them or they're just wrong?

Yet, we must also have the influences of the Stellar Minds, their perceptions, and experiences. They must represent a major force amongst these human experiences. To understand the nature of these unseen influences requires an understanding of their relationship to the physical experience here.

Why are such dramatic influences unseen in the first place? Well, they are unseen because the ability for us to see anything on the Earth has to do with the light energy and its interaction with what we know as physical matter. Without getting too technical with physics here, we can say that we see things because of how light gets absorbed or how light gets reflected by objects. The detected narrow bandwidth of visible light then limits our perception of reality.

If light gets absorbed, then the object we are observing will appear black, meaning there is an absence of light. If it reflects the light, then we see that light coming back to us.

The precise way in which variations of reflection and absorption of the light play together will provide us various details of the object being seen before us. Physicists will use an instrument called a mass spectrometer which measures the light coming from a substance while it is being burned. In this way, they can tell what elements make up the substance by comparing known spectral responses to the table of elements.

How it absorbs light has to do with the frequency of the energy of the atoms of matter. If the energy of the object is similar in frequency to the light frequency streaming towards the object, then the light will get absorbed. If it is not similar in frequency, then it will get reflected. Humans see things as they are because they only see the reflected light.

The nature of the frequency of energy here corresponds harmonically to the frequency of the energy of consciousness in heaven. Here, we mean that the harmony of the energy moves together and enjoys a good relationship, like notes sung together in a quartet of singers. The notes are pleasing to the ear if in harmony and they sound terrible if they are out of harmony.

As all the frequencies of vibration of consciousness blend in an almost infinite number of ways, matter as we know it will appear to manifest as a physical reality. The Stellar Minds created in their fall from the One, very complicated patterns of consciousness developing these energies with greater and greater density. The last concentration of these energies, in true reality, is called the Astral. Beyond that, the reflection of the astral consciousness generates the dream matrix of the physical reality we know here as Earth. Everything from the Astral is a dream or illusion. We perceive the illusion as real. Even the human body is not real, only its astral counterpart is real.

Another aspect has to do with the eye's ability to see the spectrum of light, meaning contrasts of light and dark and color. The spectrum of visible light received by the human eye is narrow. Other animals can see more ranges of light than the human being such as in the wolf, for example. All creatures have a varying ability to perceive the details of surroundings in their environment.

There is a greater range of light in the Astral than perceived by any human on the Earth unless that human has Astral vision or 'far' sight. This kind of vision is for those who have visions, possess clairvoyance (the ability to see beyond the moment or beyond normal experience). They can also see the energy around the body called the aura.

The last important element in this interplay of perception is the brain. The eyes pick up light signals and they convert them inside the brain to electrical signals, then the mind interprets these as the visible scene in view. Lest we not forget, there are other areas of perception also, sound as in hearing, tactile as in touch, flavor as in taste and odor as in smell. These five levels of the senses make up the entire experienced environment. Or do they?

Another area of perception is the extrasensory, or psychic, sense. They looked at it upon with some disdain, considered by most to be imaginary. There is ample evidence, via the experiments by Dr. Rhine at Duke University, that verifies this ability in some humans. Another sensory perception which is not acknowledged is instinct. Instinct is a rather basic bodily function relating to the animal part of us that operates below normal conscious recognition. Here, we refer to that sense that one feels when another person approaches from behind. The hackles may go up showing their presence is near.

Even with these senses, we still may not experience everything around us. There is a certain filtering going on inside our minds that blocks our ability to experience our entire environment. This happens because the mind is an efficient thinking machine. It will try to organize information into smaller and less cumbersome, less space consuming packets that go into our memory. It does this through what is called heuristic analysis. By examining previous information and comparing that information with present information, the mind seeks to find similarities.

If at least seventy percent is perceived to be similar, the mind will determine that the entire experience is identical, then ignore any new experience all together, including the additional thirty percent. They call this subliminal perceptual discrimination, or filtering. It happens often from habitual behavior, meaning all the habitual patterns we create in our life. This happens because, like our minds, we look to shave unnecessary actions from our daily routine, all in favor of providing more time for other things we might want to do. We all try to eliminate tedium when we can.

This behavior, in and by itself, doesn't seem so bad, but it contributes to and eliminates the possibility of experiencing something new out of convenience. It is possible to conclude from this; we are dreaming life seventy percent of the time, meaning we are reliving every day with what we already know and have experienced. This phenomenon bleeds over too many other aspects of human experience, such as the emotional state, which relates to a sense of safety. The effect is to dull the senses. Ideas, beliefs, and traditions become so entrenched with familiarity, we tend not to disturb or introduce anything new in our experience. We want everything comfortable and the same. Learning something new, or experiencing the unexpected, is troublesome, shocking and creates stress. This is especially true if that new idea reflects negatively on the structure of life that we spent our entire lifetime building or learning, representing a major part of our sense of safety.

We spent our early life waiting when we reach that point when we can stop learning new things and rely on what we already know. This truth makes developing new and higher consciousness a difficult path for the children of the fallen. It leads to an impossible task for the Stellar Mind to regain what it lost. This also makes the task more difficult for the One.

When something happens in our Earthly experience that

seems beyond human intervention, we attribute the phenomenon to an act of God. Floods, hurricanes, tornadoes, earthquakes, etc., all fall outside the possibility of human intervention and that also comes along with a sense of fate for those less inclined to believe in a supreme being. Fate is a curious belief. It springs out of a helpless attitude that the major events that can influence our lives are unchangeable, such as death and taxes. Though this is a cliché, it represents two very scary things we try not to think about. Fate relates to an event that represents a misfortunate circumstance. Another example of fate is when circumstances will bring two people together, which would not have otherwise happened. The most important aspect about fate is that it undermines the hope that change is possible. Given what we have learned about the One's realm, we conclude that this belief comes from our 'friends', the Djinn.

There cannot be fate if one believes one has control over one's destiny. Destiny and fate go together like bread and butter. So, we conclude that fate, like destiny, must rule out in this realm of self-responsibility. The author believes these concepts of fate and destiny are distortions of the cosmic law of cause and Effect. If they set a cause of motion, the effects must unfold from that cause. The difference is one cannot change a cause set into motion, but one can institute a new cause, which has different effects that can mitigate or override the effects of the original cause. If this were not true, then all this that has been created by the One for the benefit of the fallen to recover would mean nothing and would do nothing to change the outcome.

With quantum mechanics and the new string theory, there is sound reason to believe that consciousness moves closer to being linked to the manifestation of this physical reality. The next step in this perception of strings is more challenging. Try to consider the possibility that this reality is an illusion. This physical place is no more real than our dreams. In fact, when brain activity is analyzed between someone dreaming and someone experiencing reality, there is little difference. The last line of defense for determining madness and sanity is the 'correct' relationship and interpretation of our reality. The suggestion that our reality is not real leaves a great sense of insecurity. It smacks of mental instability. What can we rely on if we accept nothing is real? Perhaps the better answer to this lies in things and their true purpose that come into play together. Situations and the objects in our reality are more like stage props, which we can use to play out circumstances, even though they are not in real life. We can learn from these props and circumstances in the way of insights, inspiration and tough lessons springing forth from our misconceptions about the situations and the 'physical' props.

We do not deal in our attitude about circumstances and objects appearing in our dreams with because we accept the nature of dreams as being unreal. Perhaps we could adopt the same attitude about the dreaming we do in our waking state.

This new attitude could open other possibilities for our reception of new information from heaven. It is more than likely that the One is still trying to correct our perceptions of reality through the sun's light (the solar orb) even today. It is also likely that new spiritual concepts, such as, the truth about our history and the reality of who we are and where we came from is being delivered to any of those that can perceive it through an extraordinary or extrasensory perception, and for the benefit of all the others who cannot. These people might be the prophets of today. There is nothing to say that as prophets arose in the past to relay messages from the One, prophets could arise today to relay new messages from the One now.

The reason for the lack of public display of prophetic words from the One is because of the condemnation of the church around these sorts of activities. They consider all such divinations the work of the devil! The term 'devil' has nothing to do with Luxcius. It relates to the energy which the pagans used throughout history to accomplish things, identified by the many gods and goddesses in nature that defined those specific energies. Many spiritual systems that exist outside the church today suggest pieces of ancient knowledge. This knowledge may represent fragments of the keys to the kingdom as remnants of the knowledge that Mary the Magdalen provided from her relationship to and being an Initiate of Jeshua. The church condemns this idea and decrees as heretical today.

Many of the Qumran texts (the Dead Sea scrolls) the church keeps hidden, the forbidden scrolls from the Nazareans of Mount Carmel under wraps in the Vatican library. A select group of scholars reviewed only a few of those scrolls (about seven in all) for translation and made available to the public.

The author believes that these hidden scrolls, the heretical gospels according to the Gnostic traditions, may contain important information that would have been crucial to our spiritual development.

Though this work reveals much about the origins of man, and the history of the One, it still does not reveal the secrets to enlightenment, the keys to the kingdom, that Mary and others might have known and passed along. The divine quest for the Holy Grail (Mary the Magdalen) is the quest for the keys of enlightenment. Another element influencing our reality here is the Earth moves through space around the sun, but it is also moving along with our sun revolving around a larger, more distant sun, Vega. They call this movement the solar phalanx. The time of this great circle represents twenty-five thousand years of Earth's time to complete. This great circle, known among Esoteric and Gnostic groups throughout history, divides into twelve parts of two-thousand-year spans called houses. For those who are familiar with astrology, you will recognize the term. They named these phases or segments of the great circle for the twelve constellations governing them. Each house has a particular vibration of experience attributed to each constellation. it is unnecessary to talk about all the houses and their qualities in this treatise, so we will just talk about the last house we left and the house we are in now as an example. The previous house was under the influence of Pisces and that is the sign of the fish. The present house is the sign of Aquarius, the water bearer.

Each house defines the qualities of experience of the lessons being brought into the Earth realm from spirit in that time, like spices that flavor the food that we taste, such as salty, sweet, sour, spicy, and bitter. As one house switches to another house, in between each phase, the effect of the switch causes a compression period of about two-hundred years. During the compression period, time speeds up. Events will also seem to unfold quicker with faster effects. Imprints who will incarnate during this time will learn more and develop more quickly, so this is a desirable time to incarnate. From 1818 to 2018 represents the compression between Pisces and Aquarius.

The striking difference between the two periods is the 'watery' influence in our way of perceiving things: softer, clearer, and more fluid. For an example; our ideas of physics over the last century have gone from hard particle theory to soft quantum theory. Science has become comfortable with more of the imaginary than hard evidence. Besides the change in our perceptions with our ideas of reality, the vibration has also increased, making the Earth vibration closer to the astral vibration. This will mean the veil is thinner, making it possible for the average person to see, not unlike the psychic medium has seen in the past. Strange things can appear which can be more startling, which is a further challenge to our beliefs about impossibilities. The last aspect of the human body that has its correlation in heaven is the human endocrine system. These are the ductless glands within the body. These glands secrete hormones and enzymes into the body systemically, which have a major influence on how the body functions. For example, the adrenals provide sped up energy production for emergencies when the body performance must explode.

There are seven glands in all. They all exhibit a broad range of influence with the state of consciousness. The pituitary governs the growth within the body, but sometimes, as it relates to the pineal gland, its glandular secretions can alter the perception of reality directly. The pituitary has tissue that is magnetically sensitive and allows certain ranges of ultraviolet light into the system, a necessity for emotional and psychological health.

In places where the sun's light does not shine on the earth for six months at a time, such as in the north polar regions of Alaska, Greenland and Nova Scotia, inhabitants of those areas cause the depletion of these glandular substances and results in depression, lacking impetus to live life fully.

The interesting thing about the endocrine glands is they have no direct ducts to supply their secretions. Their secretions enter the system directly and systemically. So, their nature and function do not seem to be tied directly to the program of the body structure and its functions, but more indirectly influencing performance on all levels.

The pituitary and pineal glands normally work harmoniously to provide guidelines for living life in this illusionary physical world. But part of the construct of these glands and the others sits in the body dormant, silently waiting for further stimulation in more advanced ways, which could provide insights and divinations about life everlasting and other worlds outside of this prison.

This secret quality of these glands handles consciousness beyond this physical prison. They're more esoteric or Gnostic name is called 'the third eye.' I also referred these attributes to in the secret schools of Egypt as the 'left eye of Horus'. What is not commonly known except for what was taught in the halls and temples of secret brotherhoods that guard these teachings for the future of humanity when it becomes ready is that these glands can be made to vibrate on a higher frequency. A secret tradition of practice among Gnostics stimulates higher vibrations in the endocrines that allow for new and unknown hormones and enzymes to flood into the system, making it possible to experience an all-new reality.

Unfortunately, most of these teachings were destroyed by the assault of the Roman soldiers on the magnificent library of Alexandria, or just lost to antiquity.

What they promote today is the fragmented and often incorrect ways and means for humans to ascend to the higher realms. These fragmented techniques that are impotent in their own way are sharply curtailed by the changes made to humans in their original state before the Homo-Sapien-Sapien development.

Spiritual development is in the main impossible here! In fact, the insidious component to these alterations is a false presentation of spiritual development. It is another illusion to dissuade the curious seekers by providing a fake realm of pleasant and comforting reality called 'Nirvana'. Not unlike the usurped re-incarnational process that binds the human to this prison, Nirvana is the false prophet of spiritual development that keeps the rogue element of seekers from ever truly escaping by this false promise of enlightenment.

It is shocking perhaps to learn that one's chances of escaping this 'hell on earth' are none. Though, however unlikely, the only chance is to avoid the re-incarnational loop that is intrinsic here.

That is what Jeshua meant when he said, "you must give up your life, in order to have everlasting life." He was fully aware of what was going on here. But he was bound to speak in parables and riddles because he knew that direct transmission of the truth was not possible.

The real purpose of this work is to reveal the truth of the situation and offer an awakening to the dilemma so that the reader can discern for themselves that they must consider being free.

All the information that is touted now in the media, such as on 'YouTube' to be the truth and colored by including fear and hopelessness that is promoted along with it. Some of what they say is true, but it is not presented to help the seeker, but to take advantage of the fear and foreboding and raise themselves up as the 'ones' who are knowledgeable, to further their self-aggrandizement and to make a living off their suggested 'donation plates', not unlike the church.

The 'soul' is not eternal, contrary to popular religious belief. That it is eternal conflicts with the idea they must save it! Its eternal quality springs forth from the idea that the 'soul' is part of 'God'. The God they are referring to is Yahweh or Jehovah, who was also an Anunnaki deity professing this false doctrine. Jehovah can say this because of the genetic breeding involving the DNA of the Anunnaki blood mixed in with the humans (Homo-Erectus into Homo-Sapiens) by the Anunnaki geneticistIsis and Enki. In a manner of speaking, the overlords have construed this 'truth' to establish their control over the masses. The 'soul' is their twist on the collected conscious experience on Earth.

Another point in religion associated with this idea is while the 'soul' is purportedly eternal, it is not confirmed as eternal until sanctified by divine decree. They state this as; upon arrival at the gates of heaven, the 'soul' may enter and live there forever if accepted! This is the hope and general concept held by most people of faith for an afterlife. The church further confirms and allows this false idea to be true. They want to keep the human believers under their control by fear of retribution through the loss of the 'soul'. This afterlife idea is a major misconception and is simply not true!

The purpose of the imprint's experience here was more relevant than sitting on a cloud as a 'soul', with the head surrounded by a 'halo' while playing music on a harp. The faithful choose to believe in a heaven where that happens. It taught them that by 'being good' on Earth' they secured their position in their heaven. It can also be a method to create mass obedience and thus a perfect autocracy, where the chosen few (The priesthood) control the rest.

The original purpose of reincarnation was to become physical. With each incarnation, it mixed with the creation of an animal body, the human being. Through its choice of human experience, it reacts and hopefully learns from the experience. The purpose of this was to develop greater insight and memory recall.

The Highest God emanates an energy throughout the quantum, the Life Force. The purpose of the Life Force here on the Earth (the Akasha) was to record human experiences as a reference for the fallen. These recordings (akashic records) helped restore the fallen consciousness out of the dream here. Its purpose was to return the fallen from the chaos created by the disintegration into sub-consciousness. It would keep amassing human experiences into the akashic record until sufficient awareness emerged and realized. This realization is called ignition.

Ignition is a state of avalanched awareness that keeps developing into higher forms of consciousness. The avalanche becomes a chain reaction that sparks an urge to awaken out of the dream state. This is only part of the problem. The 'prodigal son' is a key biblical metaphor here. The fallen have withdrawn from the One and her realm. They took their inheritance with them into the lower worlds they created. They lost or squandered all their inheritance (their consciousness). The fallen are now lost and ashamed to return to the light worlds. If this story is familiar to biblical readers, then take note about the brother who stayed back tending to the One's realm and became angry and jealous when the One celebrates the return of the lost, as when the unfallen grew angry with the One over the fallen. Jealousy becomes a thorn in the heart of her realm and may eventually give rise to a second war in heaven over it. Some of the unfallen will side with Luxcius. They share that feeling of anger out of their jealousy. Sowing jealousy and discontent are Luxcius' intent to keep the children of the fallen downtrodden. It is not just the Djinns that are at fault here. The matter of the Earth becomes more important as the role of the children of the fallen grows. It was imperative that the children of the fallen come to realize the truth of the situation.

Thousands of years ago, Methuselah lived to be older than nine hundred years and had many children. This raises an interesting question. Why life was so much longer before? Now humans relegate to three-score and ten, or seventy to one-hundred years today! The point of the Akasha was to store up experiences for a reincarnating imprint to awaken more quickly.

Then it stands to reason, reincarnating fewer stores, less experience. Shorter life spans mean quicker returns and, therefore, greater experience stored. So, the Anunnaki modification to limit the life span was fine with the One. When consciousness rises in an imprint, an awakening can begin. The body does not keep up, though. The Anunnaki limited the ability of the body to sustain higher consciousness. This is because of an altered genetic structure in the body and changes to the amygdala in the brain to increase fear and resistance to any changes.

Esoteric circles are always engaged in spiritual practices of all sorts. They spend a great deal of effort trying to increase the body's ability to sustain and keep spiritual consciousness. They believe they achieved it through several pathways; First, is spiritual asceticism, such as abstaining from foods considered 'heavy' like meat. They replace the meat with a vegetarian diet considered being 'lighter'. Second, they restrict crude behavior personally, or not engaging with others less inclined to spiritual life. (An example is a monastic life). These paths all lead to the elimination of desire.

Desire gets depicted as the 'bad influence' here. The way of a fakir, who inflicts torture on the body, to minimize the sensitivity of the body to desire. The practice of yoga, to develop control of the mind, then subsequently over desire.

In 'death' or transition, there are two important states of being. First is the shift from the physical body. All physical sensations of the body are gone. The imprint has all its experience from the life pattern stored in the akashic record from a daily upload occurring every night. But the imprint only remains for a short time, roughly three days after the transition. (Therefore, there is the Jewish custom is to sit in Shiva for the dead for three days). Second, the Astral component of the imprint is free of the body permanently until the main body of awareness is called to the path of reincarnation.

During physical sleep, the situation is quite different. The Astral body component of the imprint leaves the body, makes its daily deposit in the akasha, then goes to the astral realm for the night, which may or may not be remembered as a dream. The caveat is the astral component must return to the physical body upon awakening the next day. Long periods of astral body separation from the physical body are unusual. Monks have remained out of body for weeks and sometimes months and rumored even for years in some special cases.

In the Taoist spiritual practice, the devotee spends countless hours meditating with special formulas that are supposed to work alchemically to give birth to a spiritual body when then ascends to heaven. Oddly enough, all that meditation can crystalize the energy into a kind of stone material. The Taoist monks revere the aspirant if when the body is exhumed by fire, they search the remains for this 'spiritual stone' and if found, they place it in a special chamber above in their meditational stupas as inspiration for others to meditate.

We do not collate the experiences of the imprint until 'death' or transition. There is the need to collate and prepare the ultimate form of the information/experience for uploading to the akashic record.

Preparation involves the elimination of the shock of the transition from all physical experience. The shock puts a twist on all the information. The shock component is an inappropriate vibration for the Akasha. That shock contains fear and mistrust. Once the imprint releases this shock and is steadied, it will dissolve, and the life force (animating spirit as the astral body) returns to the incarnational pathway. (What have some called the tunnel of light?)

What happens to the imprint containing the personality after? It's gone! It's like removing a piece of software from a computer before we shut it off. This is a crude example, but it is an accurate metaphor. If we maintain this metaphor, we loaded the imprint into the akasha like software and returns to a permanent memory. An oversight property built into the akasha determines the new life pattern of the new imprint. A 'programmer' would consider the usefulness of the software toward a task and perhaps improve upon it. The imprint does not have to survive. The animating spirit as we returned energy to the quantum of the void. However, the imprint reflection remains in the akasha in its full capacity for aliveness. We animate it as the personality of the individual. It is conscious in the akasha as though nothing had changed. It is not like a static record as you would think of it. One could go there and have a full autonomous conversation with the imprint personality. It is spontaneous there. The imprint sort of survives transition in this case and for all time. In this way, it achieves a measure of immortality. There are now built in 'permanent cycles' created for an imprint's return here on the Earth.

There is a false hope perpetrated in this. That false hope suggests a correlation of the return to the One, sharing in Her evolution and Her realm. It's a grand lie of monumental proportions! They encouraged the animating spirit to re-enter the incarnational path to serve those in control on the earth. The incarnational system that now operates on Earth is no longer Her creation. That system isn't connected to her realm at all. The only one that is served in all this is Luxcius. Here, all roads lead to him!

To go back 'home' to heaven is perhaps what everyone wants. From the day that one grows up and then leaves home, a subtle stress is created, a subtle loneliness and a reminder of the feeling of having lost one's familial embrace. It's that closeness and a sense of safety that is felt when returning home after the storminess of the day's adventures. When living life with all its difficulties, one feels a certain weariness that looms over everything, even during the good times. One becomes tired and longs for rest. We expect retirement to satiate this feeling after spending at least half of a lifetime working, but it does not. Many people feel unrest during their retirement. This unrest gets deeply seated.

It is why when one meets their so-called 'soul' mate, a certain sense of satisfaction or feeling of deeper quietness and peacefulness comes over them. Meeting one's 'soul' mate completes a part of the self that is indescribable. Yet there is another meeting, a meeting of the twin. This becomes even more satisfying but is also rare. 'Soul' mating is more common. So, what is the difference?

To understand the difference, we need to reflect on the imprint behavior here on the Earth. The imprint represents the culmination of previous experience from past incarnations as markers. The markers create a projection of some aspect that is missing in the imprint. It is called and returns to the next incarnation on Earth to find it.

The One and the new incarnation of the imprint worked together before to create a bridge of longing. The bridge to the One gets cut off now. So, the imprint keeps looking for something that is missing. The aspect which is missing is part of the One's awareness that is lost. Anything that reminds one of something familiar through an imprint's experiences here can feel welcoming. It reassures and reinstates a feeling of peace. 'Soul mating' could be temporary because of celestial influences that were once aligned but now no longer align.

A 'soul mate' represents an imprint that came from another similar imprint pattern. The other imprint was next to its own fallen element from the original form of the One. The original form of the One was crystalline before the expansion into the formless and into many Stellar Minds. When the One's original form was a crystal, it would have been two facets of the crystal adjacent or next to each other, or as a singular facet. It would be two qualities that worked closely together, so when their 'souls' (imprints) come together through an incarnation, a subtle memory of the joining returns.

It was a sense of belonging that would not otherwise emerge between two people attracted to each other for other reasons. Their relationship on Earth would be deeper and more rewarding. It would not matter whether it is between a man and a woman or between two friends, either female or male, but very often the joining does not hold and disintegrates.

Soul twinning is another story. Twinning arises as a possibility when an imprint would reach a point after many male and female lifetimes where the imprints have reached a culmination of awareness. Greater consciousness emerges on both the male and female parts. There would be sufficient male and female consciousness to allow the re-emergence of the androgynous state, the joining of male and female. When the pinnacle male and pinnacle female meet on the Earth one last time, there is a sense of greater satisfaction and completion, though it is not a done deal. The reason for joining is to work out the last vestiges of separateness left over from previous lives. If that occurs, then the fallen would return to their rightful position within the One's realm.

Twinning is rare. It occurs during the close of a compression period between two houses, such as between Pisces and Aquarius. This represents a significant change within the realm. This alters and causes the entire realm of the One, to develop again according to the quality which gets added from the re-instatement.

The state of the individual imprint's heart on Earth is a critical factor in the return. It can be said that every imprint is in varying states of "closedness." The condition of every human heart experience three knots; the knot of pride, the knot of greed, and the knot of fear. They weave together as one ball of chaos and bound with the polarized feelings generated by the energy and power of our sexual life force. This means that the individual identifies with each feeling as it relates to its survival and continuation here. Until these feelings are unpolarized by personal work, the heart has no chance to open and trust to love unconditionally. The result is the ongoing chaos and endless cycle of illusion and suffering from the apparent loneliness experienced during life on Earth.

The church's guideline for human behavior gets divided. They often disagree about the right use of will implement a

The Law of Octaves

deliberate and worthwhile spiritual life here. On the one hand, some say that it is by 'works' or 'good deeds' which represents the only way to heaven. While the other purports that 'faith' and 'devotion' alone is the only way to heaven. The issue polarizes them, which suggests they do not understand the underlying principles involved. You could say it is by 'works and faith' that could determine the increased vibration of the imprint. To at least understand this, they need to learn and comprehend the Cosmic Law of Octaves and how it affects human existence here.

It is the 'accurate definition of works and faith' that is important if life lived here is to be harmonious. You can say they reflect two aspects of the same energy. In life, the energy flow of reality follows a cosmic law that defines how the energy manifests and flows. There is a male quality which is propulsive, and a female quality which is receptive. The third quality binds them into balance and is neutral.

We can express the energy of octaves as tones played upon a piano. We tune the strings to the natural frequencies of nature or the diatonic scale. If the strings defining a seven-tone natural and unadjusted scale get played, the relationship becomes revealed. If one thumps the Do string, the energy radiated will affect and make the Re and Mi strings vibrate because of their harmonic and limited resonant relationship related to their relative string lengths.

The strings are not the same length, so their harmonic relationship diminishes the energy shared proportionately, according to their distribution. This means as the energy transmits to the next string that is shorter, only a portion of the energy will make the next string vibrate. So, it vibrates less. Then the energy progresses to the next shorter string, which reacts to the energy even less. There is a half tone interval between the third and fourth string, and between the seventh string and next octave string or Do 2. This means there is no harmonic relationship between these strings. The energy will not naturally affect the next string between the Mi string and the Fa string, or the Ti string and the Do 2 or octave string. Someone must thump again the Fa string if the progression is to continue naturally toward the Ti string.

By metaphor, they can also show the octave principle displayed on the piano in human behavior. Someone could go through life starting something new (the Do string) with a lot of enthusiasm. Their effort will continue to progress with less and less energy until it reaches an abrupt halt (the Mi string). At that point, the endeavor will either change direction, or it will just stop. Then another endeavor will start (changing direction), and they will abandon the original endeavor (this is another Do string).

To move the effort to the next level, one needs to create a shock either on the outside or inside by the right use of will (by works) overcoming the resistance encountered at the Mi-Fa point. Otherwise, they will go through life repeating the Do-Re-Mi cycle without ever accomplishing the goal of the octave.

With the second interval, it reflects the Ti-Do2 point, allowing forces beyond one's control (by faith) to affect the completion of the octave. This requires not an act of inner or outer will, as in the first case, but an act of faith in the higher order of things, or the Highest God. The balance comes from knowing when one is at the Mi-Fa point, or the Ti-Do2 point. The way to tell is when nothing can be done that will change the situation. Then they are at the Ti-Do2 point and need to allow the outcome by divine decree.

This makes up the right understanding of the work and faith issue in relationship to the right emotional development and other issues in one's life. Another term that gets introduced here is ignition. This is an important term regarding the prospect of understanding spiritual development. Ignition relates to a condition of the imprint/body when the imprint vibrates as a singularity or single frequency. The body tissues must respond in like kind when all the cells vibrate at one frequency. When this occurs, an avalanche of energy accumulates like a chain reaction. A chain reaction is a term often used in nuclear physics where an example given is a room full of mouse traps with ping-pong balls attached all go off, triggered by throwing a single ping-pong ball into the room. As the ball bounces around, it will set off traps that hold and release ping-pong balls and those balls release other balls. The chain reaction is when enough traps go off to set off the entire trap set. This is an analogue model of nuclear fission.

This is like ignition! When the imprint vibrates less chaotically, it influences the body to do the same. Cell by cell, each cell shifts in frequency. Soon, more cells will vibrate together. Eventually all the cells would vibrate together, causing ignition, a condition when all the cells of the body and the imprint shift vibration to a higher frequency. This would lead to a chain reaction. There are some spiritual practices that support the idea of this phenomenon, but it remains theoretical because reaching a singularity for the human is not possible now because of the genetic changes that were made so long ago. Out of the love and grace of the One, she had sent twelve unfallen Stellar Minds to the Earth zone to provide a combined emanation of understanding of unfallen consciousness. They would rule over the twelve houses of the Zodiac. These were to remind the children of the fallen consciousness when and if they were ever to become free. Then they would have a role model to learn from. If they were to awaken, the influence of these unfallen would have a greater impact on the thoughts, feelings, and actions to lead the children of the fallen onto the spiritual path and out of the rebirth cycle. In the Apocrypha (the Revelation) scripture by John, we are told that in the end times, we would know because there "would be wars and rumors of war, Earthquakes would happen everywhere and volcanoes would erupt everywhere, financial chaos would occur, and objects would fall to Earth. All of this would happen at the same time. Humankind would turn away from spirit in favor of materiality." Everyone is much more aware of the precarious nature of life on the Earth now. There is even talk of the 'end times. As this thought arises, the idea of the end of the world comes with it. If anyone carefully studies the words, it really means "the end of the system of things", not the end of the world. That comes later. The system of things here on the Earth defines the economic and political burden that everyone lives under.

The credit/debit system binds and enslaves everyone to experience fear of not having what they need when anyone wants it. That makes them borrow against their future. That destroys the pleasure of living freely because of the fear of losing all that one gained while the future gets mortgaged! This evil system enslaves everyone, controlling everyone's life and keeping the fear going while under absolute control. Doesn't this sound familiar? The Djinn control much of the activity, here shifting beliefs from trust and unconditional love to fear and greed, living without freedom of will and the right to pursue happiness as they deem fit.

They would need to let go of their demand to satisfy their childish cravings and deal with the deficit inside. Then they could reinstate their insolvency and walk away from this evil credit system. Then they could learn to use their energy more effectively and this would help them live more harmoniously.

The 'One World Order' plan by the Cabal (the shadow government) seems inevitable! The Cabal wants to unite as one Earth, one people, as citizens of the Earth, but with conformity, not with diversification and cooperation. Their plan requires a lot less population. They want to reduce the earth's population from 7 billion to 500 million! Why would one ask? First 500 million is a size that is easier to control. It also means essentials such as food and water would be easier to manage for the multitudes. But Loving each other because we are all in life together would not be tolerated. Their plan involves a fascist regime or autocracy.

    If everyone could come together in the right way, they would not struggle to be alive but live life as one family, a family of humankind, with abundance. The belief there is not enough to go around is a barefaced lie. They perpetrate it to instigate conflict and disorder. If you examine growth in nature, you will find abundance within that growth. Is it no wonder that they engineer the food without the abundance of the seed, which promises our continued abundance? For every seed that grows makes a hundred more insuring our continued existence. They twist the truth by controlling the seed and thus control life and death here.

The Arcturian/Sirian Gambit

It is strange to hear and embrace that the Earth is far from being isolated in the galaxy. We know the Earth for its rich mineral deposits and water as a remnant of the way Tiamat used to be. Several alien races who came there mined Tiamat, exploiting the minerals present for their use and for profit. Then the calamity of Nemesis' orbital planet (a member of the dwarf sister star) came into the solar system and crashed into Tiamat, destroying both planets. Those alien races stayed away until the dust settled. The remnant of Tiamat found its new third orbit around the sun from the original 5thorbit with only a third of Tiamat remaining. The rest of Tiamat exists as the ring of asteroids between Mars and Jupiter.

785,000 years ago, the first to return here were the Arcturians. Much of the planet was missing, but water got added to balance the planet after rotation on its own axis got established. The deepest trench in the ocean today (the Mariana trench) represents the original rip from Tiamat. Why this trench exists today still puzzles scientists.

    The only survivors of the debacle of Tiamat's destruction were the Nome-Lu-Lu who sought refuge near the core of the planet within deep natural cave structures. Then later, Arajixx introduced new life on the remnant planet. It developed first in the oceans and later the surface, along with flying creatures in the new atmosphere.

    The Arcturians were interested specifically in minerals found in this quadrant of galactic space. Tiamat was rich in these minerals, which they used for their huge ship construction and their formidable weaponry. Even today, many species know them throughout the galaxy as ferocious fighters possessing the most advanced weapons.

The Arcturians, disappointed to learn the fate of their favorite mining planet now obliterated by a planetary collision. They gave the order to stay clear of the area where Tiamat used to be because the ring of dangerous asteroids was dashing about wildly between Mars and Jupiter.

The Nibiru system returned to the aphelion of its elliptical orbit for another 3600 years, leaving this solar system to stabilize.

Luxcius realized the calamity might create doubt from the One about his choice for a suitable planet. His rehabilitation plan needed a suitable planet, but this unforeseen mishap did not persuade Luxcius to change his choice of location. After Arajixx adjusted the remains with water and stabilized the planet with its spin, Luxcius figured the disaster was past and no longer a concern. Luxcius did not reveal this problem to the One. He could still use the remains of Tiamat for his original purpose. After several hundred thousand years, the new planet, much smaller than Tiamat, became Earth. The evolution of primates on the land mass would be the perfect choice as hosts to the fallen.

Meanwhile, Luxcius was unaware that there were eight surviving Nome-Lu-Lu living inside the planet's core. Luxcius' androgyny debacle of the fallen made him abandon the project after being scorned by the One. Angry with the One, he vowed to get revenge and went off to Aldebaran to sulk. There he considered future efforts to thwart the One's plan for the fallen. The Arcturians explored other systems for their much-needed mineral deposits. One system was in the Draco star system. Gamma Draconis. Three planets revolved around that star system, which was populated with a reptilian race. Atanin Prime was the center of their culture. One feature of that culture's activities was slave trading. The Arcturians often experienced skirmishes with other cultures. They wanted dominance of the mineral deposits on those systems they invaded. Their armies had become depleted, and they needed fresh troops. So, they negotiated the purchase of several hundred thousand reptilians to fill the ranks.

After many hundreds of years, these trained reptilians functioned as their front-line warriors. The Arcturians still treated them as slaves, much like the gladiators of Rome. But their fighting would be for the Arcturian empire. The Arcturians decided it was time to return to Tiamat/Earth. They wanted to investigate the resurgence of mineral mining possibilities. Upon scouting the situation on the new Tiamat/Earth planet, their scanning equipment revealed pockets of minerals buried deep inside the mantle. This required extensive tunneling. They landed with special sound drills and bored into the Earth's mantle in the region where Tibet now sits. Once the tunnels were created, they sent in the soldier reptilians to collect the much-needed rare Earth elements.

After several hundred years passed, the Arcturians were drawn away to one of their other occupied territories. This territory was a mining colony in the Mica star system. A rebellion took place and needed to be suppressed. They left one of the reptilian generals, Gandoor, in charge of the Earth to continue the mining operations. General Gandoor became the Arcturian slave overseer. The rebellion spread through-out many mining colonies in the Mica system. The Arcturians engaged with the rebels for thousands of years. Meanwhile, on Earth, Gandoor realized the Arcturian masters would not be returning to Earth. So General Gandoor took the greater role of leadership over the slaves, and like Spartacus, who led the slaves against Rome, Gandoor declared Earth as their own sovereign planet. They continued to mine in preparation to negotiate a trade for their freedom should their masters return. The reptilians lived in the tunnels and rarely approached the surface. They continued with their sound boring tools until they uncovered the eight Nome-Lu-Lu. The Nome-Lu-Lu had entered a suspended state and appeared to them as a large crystalline structure. The reptilians could not comprehend or understand this structure, but they sensed an importance about the structure and chose not to disturb it and continued to build their nest all around it. After several thousands of years passed, the surface world continued. The Lemurian culture developed out of the water element with advanced mental capacities on the eastern coast of the new island continent called Mu or Lemuria. The Atlantean culture developed also on the land and their evolution continued the other part of the island continent called Atlan. This would later become Atlantis. Meanwhile, in the Orion binary star system, Sirius A and Sirius B became unstable. Luxcius' new plan involved destroying the female of the Orion population through the toxic radiation emitted by the unstable stars. This forced the Sirians to leave their system to seek a new home and a solution to their apparent genocide. Luxcius influenced the Sirians to follow a path toward Earth. This would become Luxcius' new plan to sow unrest within the fallen through conflict.

The Sirians landed in Atlantis. They surmised these Atlantean humanoids could be the answer to their genocide problem. The Sirians negotiated an exchange of advanced technology for the Atlantean females they needed for genetic altering. They carried out their genetic modifications for thousands of years until they reached a desired compatibility to their own kind. Once this got accomplished, they left the Earth. Those less than desirable female mutants were left behind, along with a 'skeleton crew' of Sirians to assist the Atlanteans with the use of the Sirian technology.

The new hybrid females and the rest of the Sirian race left Earth to a promising new system of planets in the Pleiades star system. They live now on one of the larger planets in that system called Pleagora. The Atlanteans rejected the remaining hybrids. They forced them to go to a colder land further north, called Hyperborea. In the Sudan, the Nile valley was fertile, and the river was wide. Then, approximately 600 thousand years ago, another alien race arrived from the Lyra star system and landed there. These beings were tall, humanoid bipedal beings that looked catlike in appearance. Though they often walked on all fours, they also stood upright. Many possessed wings and could fly. They saw this planet as a good place to colonize.

They built the sphinx along with the great pyramid, a machine they would use to facilitate easy travel to their home world. The control of the machine came from a crystalline computer that sat on top as a capstone. (That capstone is now missing)

The computer also controlled the weather in the area, creating a sprawling paradise around the Nile valley. They planned a great city to surround the Giza plateau. But to their utter surprise, the Nibiru system returned, causing the planet to wobble.

There were no collisions, but land masses became unstable and broke into smaller island continents while the red sea engulfed the Nile River and flooded the entire plain. The Lyrans abandoned their plans for colonization, realizing the instability of the planet was more than they prepared for. They left the remnants of their great unfinished city, the sphinx and their pyramid machine and never returned.

It would be the Egyptian dynasty of Khufu much later which would reshape the cat features of the sphinx's face to Khufu's likeness. Khufu also marked the great pyramid with his cartouche, (his royal symbol) claiming the artifact as his own, a trait common to Egyptian pharaohs.

Approximately 450,000 years ago, the Nemisis system returned. Nibiru, a larger planet of the system, suffered from a depleted and contaminated atmosphere from the constant stream of iron oxide from its dwarf star. The Anunnaki race who populated the planet was in near perihelion to the sun and

Earth. The Anunnaki landed on Earth, in Mesopotamia near the Tigress/Euphrates River. Chaldeans settled in the city of Ur nearby. King Anu and his two sons, Enki, and Enlil arrived to negotiate the mineral rights with the Chaldeans to mine gold from the area.

The Anunnaki enamored the Chaldeans and believed them to be gods from heaven. Their name given in Chaldean/Sumerian meant "those from on high came."
In exchange, Enlil was to teach the Chaldeans astronomy, mathematics, and physics. The Anunnaki needed the gold in large quantities to seed the atmosphere on Nibiru to resolve their atmospheric problems.

After many years in the mines, the Anunnaki miners, known as the Egigi complained that the mining work was too much and refused to re-enter the mines. King Anu considered the problem and realized they could make use of the indigenous tribes of humanoid creatures called Homo-Erectus. With a few genetic modifications, these humanoids would be the perfect work force needed.

Luxcius approached king Anu and influenced him to bring forth two of his best geneticists, Aset, (aka Isis) and Wepwawet (aka Enki) to alter the Homo-Erectus humanoids to recreate them as Homo-Sapiens. He also persuaded the king to alter their lifetime to 100 years and limit their consciousness and ability to develop spiritually so they would be smart enough to work the mines, but not smart enough to rebel. The fallen's chances for recovery reduced even further.

There were many squabbles between the two brothers. King

Anu planned to return to Nibiru, leaving his two sons in charge. Anu divided the territories between them. But they did not satisfy Prince Enki with that. He wanted to oversee the entire Earth. A fight ensued between the brothers. Prince Enki killed his brother, Prince Enlil. The king banished Enki from the occupation garden called Edin. Enki left Edin and headed for the lands to the North. Enki entered a place called Nod, the Hyperborean colony of Atlantean hybrids.

King Anu assigned one of his Anunnaki generals, Yahweh, to oversee the colony making sure no further difficulty would arise from Enki. Enki found the female Sirian-human hybrids in Nod extremely attractive. He invited some of the other overlords to come to Nod to see these hybrid females for themselves. Nekhen (aka Horus), Djehuta (aka Thoth) and Ahlahe (aka Allah) joined him. They copulated with the female hybrids and gave birth to the titans (the giants called nephilim). These creatures eventually spread throughout all the continents and when food for them became scarce, they became cannibalistic, eating each other and attacking the homo-erectus where they could find them.

Thousands of years later, the One became angry that they left these creatures to devour humans. Disgusted with this situation, she shifted the orbit of Nibiru closer to Earth. This caused the Earth to wobble, and the axis of the planet shifted. Massive tidal waves arose (the great flood) which almost destroyed all life on the surface except for a few survivors, but almost all the giants got wiped out.

The survivors of the colony of Nod eventually became the

civilization of Abra. This is where the overlord Yahweh would become 'god the father' of Abra-ham (the community of Abra). The twelve tribes, remnants of Abra, descended back into Assyria-Babylonia and spread throughout the middle east. The Babylonians eventually captured and enslaved some for over 500 years. Hebrews wrote their history usurping much of the Sumerian knowledge of the past, integrating it with their worship of Yahweh (aka Jehovah).

The Sumerian tablets described the fight between Enki and his brother Enlil. The Hebrews wrote their version of the story of Cain and Abel, copied from the Sumerian records during their enslavement of the Hebrew by Babylonia. Later, in Egypt, they would also write in their historical accounts that Set (aka Enki) would kill Osiris (aka Enlil).

Among the advanced technological feats accomplished by the Arcturians, is Faster-than-light speed. They accomplished this by creating a warp of time-space in the quantum field. Albert Einstein's theory of relativity established the speed of a light barrier in 1905. He proposed that as an object of a certain mass approached the speed of light, that mass would increase, making it impossible to reach the speed of light because the mass would become infinite.

Today, physicists describe space as a 'quantum field of dark matter.' This concept also involves time. So, they refer to it as space-time. Trying to go faster than the speed of light by moving a mass with increasing acceleration and energy is no longer viable. However, they realize that space-time or the quantum field has no such light speed limit. Now, they do not possess the technology to alter space-time in this way, but they are working on ways which might accomplish this.

Since the Arcturians enjoy a million years of development beyond human engineering, they move space-time many degrees beyond the speed of light. Their ships do not move relative to space but move the space relative to their ships. In this process of travel, they discovered time dilation. As a result, stable wormhole creation became another feat of their technology. This allows for the creation of portable holes that can connect one part of space-time to another part. This form of 'wormhole' travel provided instant transportation for vehicles from one point in space to another with no time passing or the need to navigate extreme distances. With some adjustments to these principles of physics, time travel became a reality as well.

They engineered the boring tools on Earth in a similar technology. By using hyper sound (light at sound frequencies), they could shift the dense molecular structure of matter beyond the regions of the nuclear binding force and turn solid rock into molten magma.

The reptilians were meat eaters, but they also crave the energy produced by emotional outbursts or intense emotional states, such as fear, anger, and anxiety. The humanoids produced these in large quantities on Earth. This elixir of extreme emotional states creates opiate like effects which then addict the reptilians.

The reptilians developed telepathy. Not unlike the Lemurians, they also could place images and thoughts into another's mind. With combined reptilian efforts, they could amass tremendous mental energy and affect the mass consciousness of an entire planet. That planet is Earth!

Many conspiracies express the theory the government has retrieved crashed UFO crafts. Some include the conspiracy that UFO occupants survived and now cooperate with governments to assist with the advancement of their human technology.

Despite misinformation placed in the public domain, since 1943, the Germans retrieved several crashed UFO crafts and back engineered those crafts. They created their own antigravity crafts called 'Hanabu'. The development of jet powered bombs like the V1 buzz bomb, jet powered fighter aircraft and the intercontinental ballistic rocket like the V2, and even the use of atomic energy was also alien inspired. These were only part of their advanced weaponry before the second world war ended. For the allies, these crafts were far superior to our own aircraft. The war ended in 1945. They did not use the Hanabu for aerial combat during the war because of political and military internal conflicts in the German High Command.

Many officers of the German High Command realized they might not win the war, despite all their superior weapons. They prepared for a secret retreat. They sent more than a hundred submarines to Antarctica. The Germans built a secret Third/Fourth Reich military base there.

Admiral Richard Byrd convinced the Navy in 1946 to send a flotilla of several warships and planes with five thousand troops to investigate the enemy operations in Antarctica. This operation got codenamed 'Operation High jump'. The Navy discovered that one hundred fifty German subs were missing from the German registry since the war ended. That evidence convinced the war department to follow up on Byrd's recommendations. The result was catastrophic. Ships and aircraft were attacked successfully by the Hanabu craft. Byrd returned having lost ships, planes, and men. He relayed a warning of the seriousness of the situation to the pentagon. No action was taken openly.

Later, the first of many crashed, we retrieved UFO crafts in the US, beginning with two that came down near Roswell in 1947. They alarmed President Harry Truman by many UFO crafts hovering over Washington one night. He created an independent panel of military and civilian personnel to oversee this national security problem. Truman would call that secret group of 12 members the 'Majestic Twelve' or MJ-12 for short. They created a new security clearance level just for these men called the 'cosmic clearance', a clearance far beyond classified or top secret. Even future presidents did not have the clearance to view the information gathered by these men.

Also, in 1945, over two hundred Nazi scientists and engineers from the Peenemunde and other rocket facilities were secretly brought over to the United States with war crimes immunity under a technology exchange program called 'operation paperclip.' Werner Von Braun led the jumpstart of the US rocket program and the secret antigravity research program. When asked how the Germans became so advanced so quickly, Von Braun explained they had help from the aliens. That group formed what we know today as NASA. Once the antigravity program began, they created a top secret black-ops military organization called the US Space Command. This group would begin plans for militarizing space.

In 1949, the grays arrived from the Zeta Reticuli star system. They came to meet with President Eisenhower at Groom Lake military base. He was officially golfing in palm springs, but they secretly took him to Groom Lake for the meeting. There, the Zeta beings offered a warning against agreeing with the tall whites of Orion. They explained that the tall whites from Orion did not have their best interests at heart. They offered their help instead, but without the additional technology help. The president declined their offer. Our military industrial complex influenced the president's decision by the persuasive arguments of national security. The military decided with the tall whites from Orion for their technological help.

The Orions, or 'tall whites', suggested a clear and present danger of future conflicts with other alien cultures. These tall whites wanted access to humans for their own experimental purposes, in exchange for their technological help. The government agreed, so long as the abductees would not remember the proposed abductions. That experimental work still goes on at several secret underground bases, like Dulce, New Mexico. They shut the secret base at Dulce down for the atrocities happening there, but after a new administration came into power, the new government reopened it.

Most of the UFO sightings are not alien craft, but back engineered craft flown by the United States Air Force. Because of their secret propulsion technology, they haven't needed the space shuttle in many years. Area 51 and site 4 are top secret research areas where the latest propulsion research is conducted. The military created the TR-3B triangular craft there, from alien technology.

For seventy years, many of the technological advancements we enjoy now are alien based, such as cell phones, lasers, transistors, integrated circuitry, nanotechnology, fiber optics, and the human genome.

Meanwhile, the reptilian race living underground, control the cabal shadow governments with mind control. The reptilians influenced the development of the HAARP grid system, affording the US with another weapon, one of weather control. The HAARP system also extended the range and intensity of the reptilian mind control wave to better control mass consciousness. In addition, they supplied the chemical formula now being sprayed overpopulated areas around the world. These sprays are called 'chem trails. This chemical particulate spray is supposed to help retard global warming by blocking the heat of the sun, but the actual reasons for its use are to retard the consciousness of the people and control the weather.

The chem-trails differ from normal vapor contrails created from the exhaust of jet aircraft. Vapor trails do not last once the vapor is gone and dissolve quickly. These trails of particulates do not dissolve and go on almost from horizon to horizon. They crisscross often to increase the dosage in an area, and they rarely pertain to normal jet traffic lanes. The Arcturians also created an invisible grid around the Earth as a kind of blockade to prevent others who might want to infringe on their claims to the minerals. After the masters left the Earth, the reptilians allowed passage through the grid when the United States wanted to send astronauts to the Moon and to Mars. The astronaut Edward Mitchell complained once in an interview. He accidentally grumbled that Buzz Aldrin kept lamenting he wanted to go back to Mars! The government put a gag order on the media to remove that statement.

In 1960, a scientist by the name of Dyson theorized that aliens might harness a sun's energy by building a mega-sphere around the sun with solar collectors, using hundreds of thousands of collecting satellites. Ever since that theory was launched, the hunt for advanced alien cultures that might create technology to do that was coupled with the hunt for suns with a peculiar light emitted from them. This discovery might show the existence of Dyson's spheres. Since that time, two such distant suns in other solar systems have been found with the strange light fluctuations, though no trace of alien activity has been found to date, or at least not made public.

Mainstream science would not advocate openly that alien civilizations are doing this. It would certainly be the very last hypothesis they would consider. Jason Wright, an astronomer from Penn State University, recently discussed the discovery of EPIC 204278916, a young star showing a massive dip in output energy by 22% over the course of a century. This was astounding! Two theories proposed at the time didn't cope adequately to explain the phenomenon. NASA's Kepler spacecraft discovered it in 2014. Ever since a team of astronomers led by Simone Scaringi from the Max Planck Institute for Extraterrestrial Physics in Germany, have been keeping tabs on its dips in light, or 'light curves'. The German team has proposed another theory that the effect was caused by the existence of a 'proto-planetary disk' of dust that's oriented 'edge-on' in relation to the Earth. That orientation could mean not only blocking the light from the star at certain times, but it could also be at the wrong angle to be viewing its own infrared radiation.

[Note to the reader:] A protoplanetary disk is a theory of a rotating dense gas and dust that would surround a newly formed star. Over 78.8 days of observations, EPIC 204278916 displayed irregular dimming up to 65% for around 25 consecutive days. Something as huge as a planet orbiting a star would cause it to dim just 1%. Two theories were proposed; first, there is a massive swarm of comets orbiting the star and second, the star is distorted and spinning so fast it becomes oblate, with a larger radius around its equator. Neither of these theories has held up to scrutiny.

Though the Dyson concept remains theoretical, the earth has such a mega-sphere around it. It extends several thousands of miles out into space. Its purpose is not to draw solar energy from a sun, but to absorb other forms of energy from the earth's surface. Here, specifically, the intense emotional energy coming from humans suffering from great fear and anxiety. The construct of this grid surrounding the earth is invisible to the naked eye normally. It can be seen if the light spectrum of the viewer is expanded, such as would be the case of an intuitive or psychically gifted observer. It is possible to see it if one relaxes their eyes without expectations. Then it may become viewable. Its appearance is very much like the pattern of the flower of life, a six-sided interwoven pattern linked with countless hundreds of thousands of other hexagonal shapes forming a tight linked grid. The grid shows a greenish color in appearance.

The purpose of the grid serves to collect emotional energy from humans on the surface of the planet, but the grid also serves as a barricade against anyone leaving entering the planet as well. The gates for this grid exist only at the poles, the largest gate exists in Antarctica.

So, when the Military Space Command of the US Airforce wants to go to their bases on Mars, they seek permission from the reptilians who control the passage through the grid. The grid also prevents any species from outside of the Earth from coming and attempt to mine the surface for their own purposes. There is a north polar orbiting alien satellite, coined the 'Black Knight'. It controls the grid and monitors the energy streaming up from the surface.

This satellite contains a great deal of advanced alien technology which the US wants. They sent the shuttle Columbia on a mission to strike the satellite and bring it out of its orbit down to the surface for examination and back engineering. The Black Knight also carries aboard advanced particle beam weapons which fired upon the shuttle when it got too close. The shuttle got destroyed, along with all the astronauts aboard. Official reports described that a mishap aboard the shuttle caused it to explode. The black Knight remains in orbit today, unaffected by any outside influences.

The US Space Command has been colonizing Mars for many years and they have a crew of military people living in domes there now. This is top secret to the public. They show publicly only sending robotic rovers to Mars until they send the 'first' manned mission in 2030.

The Earth is functioning under an alien occupation, and only a select few humans know this truth. That makes the Earth a 'prison planet' and the reptilians are in charge!

The reptilians were aware of the Nemisis/Nibiru dwarf star system and its 3600-year orbit around our solar system, and in particular, the potential for cosmic disaster. The reptilians calculated that with each elliptical orbit, gravitational forces altered the orbit slightly as the huge planet passed between Mars and Jupiter. The danger this time was more serious. The larger planet Nibiru would come nearer to the sun. Its large magnetic field would increase the electromagnetic energy on the surface of the sun, raising the temperature of the sun and giving rise to super flares. The orbit coming in was not serious, but then the orbit shifted. Nibiru's return path could have a deleterious effect on the sunspot energy and solar wind, causing a super flare and could engulf the planet.

The reptilians deliberated on the problem and realized they could not stop what would happen to the earth. They would not walk away from this treasure trove of minerals, endless supplies of flesh when needed, and the endless amount of enormous emotional energies available, all afforded them by their masters. Besides, this planet was their home now. They would not give it up.

The reptilians realized one way to circumvent the calamity was to create a temporal loop where they could capture the Earth as a matrix within the loop and separate the Earth matrix from the real Earth. The super flare destroyed so, while the real Earth, the matrix Earth would continue unaffected.

Within the time loop, they adjusted the timeline to a time before the catastrophe happen. From that time onward, they kept resetting the loop. Inside the time vault, locked away forever, earth time continued within a certain sequence that repeated endlessly.

[Note to the reader:] (Ecclesiastes 3-15 King James Version) "That which hath is now; and that which is to be hath already been and God requireth that which is past."

The reptilians had also usurped the incarnational cycle. Those who die in the loop recycle as new people, unaware of their original life under this reptilian regime. They encourage those who are dying to follow the tunnel of light. The familial apparitions are illusions given to those during transition to re-enter the loop without resistance and continue to recycle ad infinitum. To break free of this prison, people would have to choose not to enter this tunnel. They would need to avoid the tunnel and go instead into the quantum void, which would appear more difficult and scarier to do emotionally.

Those living inside the vault of the Earth matrix now will live out their lives procreating in the 'matrix' without ever knowing the truth of this secret. The 'hope' of an afterlife follows the reptilian plan while one enters the incarnational path usurped from the One Most High, emerging always as a 'new person' living a 'new' life without remembrance of the old life before, all inside the permanent prison of planet Earth. The population grows inside the loop like a farm ripe to be eternally harvested.

Approximately in the year 2294 of real time, roughly eight hundred years ago in loop time, a super solar flare destroyed the Earth. The author is writing this book while inside the temporal loop in the year 2018, 276 years before the flare strikes the world. Even though the earth was destroyed 800 years ago, the matrix earth continues inside the loop for those 800 years until the loop reset pulse and then the loop repeats endlessly.

[Note to reader:] "And men were scorched with great heat, and blasphemed the name of God, which hath power over these plagues: and they repented not to give 'him' glory." (Ref. Revelations, Chapter 16, Verse 9)

By the year 2293 of real time, several people had left the Earth to colonize Mars, Saturn and many of the moons made inhabitable beyond the inner solar system, along with huge space stations serving humans and other alien species. Those humans that escaped the earth prison became space farers, explorers, and traders. They advanced sufficiently after FTL (faster than light) drives got invented to help colonize other star systems many light years away. Those inside the temporal loop continue in ignorance of the truth of the matrix as slaves. The reptilian race controls the earth matrix. They feed on the human emotional energy and the flesh of those captured inside.

This presented an interesting problem for the One. She realized the fallen consciousness entered utter chaos and the abyss of the quantum. However, there was still Her Nome-Lu-Lu, trapped inside the Earth, inside the temporal loop. She devised a new plan; to free Her Nome-Lu-Lu and become part of a new template for a new human hybrid species of her own.

The Limited Homo-Sapien

Circumstances are better understood when the ramifications of historical events that directly shaped the evolutionary future of man become clear. Once accepted, man can improve along the evolutionary latter now, is exaggerated. It is based on false hope! It turns out ever since Homo-Erectus (an early prehistoric hominid) was captured and genetically altered with the DNA of an advanced race of beings from another world, (the Anunnaki) a new species emerged; Homo-Sapiens.

Modern anthropologists now argue that Cro-Magnon man (early modern man) is equivalent to modern man and is now renamed as Cro-Magnon-Homo-Sapien. Which means now, modern man is Homo-Sapien-Sapien.

[Note to the reader:] Sapien means wise. So, the anthropologists say that evidence reveals that Cro-Magnon man was also wise, as wise perhaps as modern man.

It might be confusing to comprehend the beginnings of a different species of hominids that mysteriously appear on the timeline of evolution on earth without a shred of evidence as to their origins.

To understand why they limited humans today, one needs to first understand what that means. When the Anunnaki changed the DNA of Homo-Erectus, the changes were so dramatic; it warranted reclassification into the Homo-Sapien level of development. On the surface, this alteration seems fantastically positive, an evolutionary leap of conscious sentient intelligence improvement.

If the details of the genetic work got revealed, then knowing those changes, the precise nature of the changes, had a

The Limited Homo-Sapien

specific purpose. Historically (ref: Sumerian codices)

Mining minerals became too laborious for the Anunnaki, so they captured primates indigenous to the area called Homo-Erectus. The Anunnaki needed a workforce that was strong, smart enough to carry out the mining tasks, but not smart enough to realize the truth of their captors. They feared they might rebel.

In the first step, they activated those aspects in the genome, reflecting the great strength and stamina required for the harsh mining conditions. But great strength was not the only attribute needed. The Anunnaki needed to teach the new hominids the use of their technology used for mining. In the second step, intelligence and greater awareness were increased by adapting the Anunnaki intelligence factors into the Hominid's DNA. Fearing that a long life might give rise to greater recognition of their plight and possible disgruntlement, they altered the cell regeneration cycle of the pineal and pituitary glands.

This limited the hominids lifespan from their original thousand-year span to one-hundred years. Though this effect could have sped up the possibility of reawakening the lost consciousness of the fallen more quickly, it also prohibited the time needed to develop the consciousness further in a single lifetime.

The condition of the original Hominid could enjoy a thousand years of perfect health, barring the unfortunate mishap of being eaten by a predator or some other fatal injury. A reduction of the regeneration cycle also caused a genetic disease called old age. The Anunnaki didn't care about that because they bred these creatures by the thousands. If one grew too old to work, they would simply replace the old one with a new younger one.

The positive aspect of all this genetic engineering would increase the number of incarnations that a hominid would experience, thus increasing the possibility for their memory to return from their original minimized awareness. The Most High did not interfere with the Anunnaki genetic work. She saw this as a supportive action for her plans.

King Anu was not happy that Enki added the greater intelligence factors of the Anunnaki to the hominids. He felt it was an unnecessary risk of rebellion. This was another reason king Anu banished Enki after he had killed his brother Enlil. This meant the king would need to add greater security forces to keep the hominids in line. He did not want to spread his ground forces too thin.

The Anunnaki would stay long enough on earth to bring the first load of gold desperately needed to protect the atmosphere of their planet Nibiru from the influence of the debris from their dwarf star. To ensure their mining would continue after they left and to protect their mines from marauders, king Anu placed his overlords in charge during their absence.

There were many mining locations throughout the earth. They gave each overlord governing power over their respective territories. Though there were border disputes that would arise later between the overlords, their hominid armies would not attack neighboring colonies out of mutual respect.

The Limited Homo-Sapien

Scripturally speaking, it explains why armies were directed at some territories but prohibited to engage in other specific military actions.

After several hundreds of years after Nibiru's return to its outer orbit, the focus on mining changed. The importance of maintaining control of their individual territories turned into advancing ambitions to gain more territory, giving rise to wars between the regional governors. This rise of ambition and aggressive behavior was an effect from Luxcius to implement his plan for the complete destruction of the children of the fallen.

I perceived as much as the shortened life span of the hominids as helpful. There were serious drawbacks from the work on the hindbrain of the hominids. With the alteration of the amygdala, the possibility for the hominid to develop was curtailed to where the hominids could not process the light building support from Sukon's energy streaming to the earth. The children of the fallen would be permanently hampered and would remain limited. This changed the One's plans.

The One holds dear her vision of freedom for all sentient beings to develop. Her trials and tribulations have not changed that vision. Her efforts have had casualties, however. Because of Luxcius's pride, arrogance, and willful disobedience, those retracted from the full consciousness of the One are lost. Their only recourse is gathering their scattered essence from the quantum field by the grace of the One Most High.

The field pervades the entire universe because the fallen had created the physical realm with their energy. Despite the concentration of remaining consciousness being extremely small, the quantum field keeps the energy. They are lost but not destroyed. The One could gather her lost from the quantum field eventually if she does so.

Luxcius thwarted the One's efforts to recover the fallen. It has not been a single action on his part. The Djinn have indirectly brought this catastrophe to bear on her efforts of expansion.

The One regretted what happened to those choosing to separate, but it provided her with renewed enthusiasm. She launched an affirmative effort to expand her way not just through the light worlds of the upper kingdom, but also for the sentient beings living in the middle and even the lower kingdoms.

The sacrifices made by her children and the energy from them in the quantum provided her greater insight and understanding. It revealed a profound perception of what is being and a quantum leap for the expression of her expansion.

She cannot persist for long in the middle or lower kingdoms.

The Cosmic Transformation

Their vibrations are intolerable to a light being. She needed candidates in both kingdoms to function as the embodiment of her awareness, harmony, and interconnectedness for her to remain in the middle and lower kingdoms long enough to develop them into her expansion.

These required beings of the middle kingdom willing to undergo a transformation, for the sake of a new species and the expansion of her way. The middle kingdom beings needed the attributes of extreme flexibility, not in the physical sense, but in the spiritual energetic sense.

The One considered the Kieralons. They are a level five species (fifth dimension), living in the Sheliac system near Vega. The Kieralon has an extremely flexible energy form and spiritually developed enough to support her expansion. They selected only two for the mission. This transformation meant a complete separation from their kind, which was extremely difficult. The Kieralon are community oriented, the village, community, and planet as a united family.

After much consideration, a Kieralon, male and female, got chosen. The Kieralon's life expectancy is approximately 20,000 Earth years. Mating occurs by arrangement between members of the community, and they join after their birthing cycle begins as mates for life. The chosen ones were the female Nala Ganalaya, and the male Jailung Prithmedea.

They were eager to serve the One Most High, but they had yet to learn the extent of the task before them. The One Most High realized the Kieralon could not sustain a lengthy time in the lower kingdoms of level three (third dimension). She needed two level three beings, also male and female, to serve as lower kingdom embodiments for her new species.

There was still the problem of the Nome-Lu-Lu locked in the reptilian temporal loop, surrounded by the nest at the center of the Earth. her choice of level three beings would need to be strong to permit the 5th level brings the opportunity to extract the Nome-Lu-Lu. Those level 3 beings would require substantial pre-life experience which supported the characteristics of loyalty, honor, devotion, and faith beyond their capacity to understand.

She scanned the temporal loop from its origin to the reset pulse, to find those that might contain larger trace amounts of fallen consciousness. They might respond to certain cues under certain conditions. She enlisted the help of an enlightened master already in service to the One Most High, who lived on Earth at level three for thousands of years in Atlantis. The One chose him as an interlocutor and guide inside the loop. His name was Yokar.

They chose well the male and female third level candidates before their birth in the loop. Yokar descended to the Earth from the seventh level (seventh dimension) to support the human male and female during their transformation.

They were tested to determine their worthiness and willingness to undergo the isolation from their familial and other human connections and facing inner issues that had their roots from the fall consciousness. She hoped to call others as well, to test them and determine if they had enough fallen awareness to further expand the project. It would be determined later that they would find no others!

The male candidate later met with Yokar and become his mouthpiece to draw in other candidates. Many years later, the female candidate awakened. Yokar touched her head while she was asleep, then she awakened to his presence, which began her path to the greater awakening.

The One designed journey to special energy locations around the world, where she influenced and examined those who would later take part. Then, Yokar took the male candidate on those journeys, while bringing hundreds of other candidates to the sacred sites. After scrutiny and testing, she could find no one to measure up to the requirements except for the chosen pair.

Years after they completed the journeys, Yokar held a last retreat in the Catskill Mountain region of New York State. It was an ultimate test to see if anyone present would respond to the spiritual call for the awakening. Yokar used the power of voice to sing a string of tones loaded with hidden messages buried within them. Only the chosen female responded to Yokar's test. The test interacted with the amygdala and the throat using those special tones and his silent messages. These were the same patterns he used in the king's chamber of the Great Pyramid during the first initiations. The One was pleased with Mary and Michael. She completely supported Yokar's confirmation of her choices for the human components in her cosmic transformation plans.

The One was aware that if the two human subjects were to be ready and able to change their bodies, they needed corrections in their brain neuron synaptic patterns. Genetic alterations were also required to lift the pre-deluvian genetic changes to their system blocking spiritual development.

She wanted scientists familiar with level three human anatomy, and the skill to remove those obstructions for their limited development established by the Anunnaki geneticists, Enki, and Isis.

She requested the expertise of two geneticists, one from Arcturus and another from Sirius. They got assigned to decode and recode the altered human DNA in the human subjects. But she suspected these two species might attempt to undermine her, so the knowledge of her suspicions was kept secret even from her closest confidant, Yokar.

Yokar was assigned as an advocate for the humans on Earth. He also oversaw their progress through this first phase of their transformation. The One wanted to use the opportunity to evaluate these nonhuman beings for their honesty, integrity, and intent. Did they support and serve her way? She gave the geneticists a chance to do what was required and not sabotage the mission by destroying the human candidates before they completed their Kieralon merger.

The Arcturians recommended an apparatus be constructed to stimulate the neural pathways and invigorate the endocrine system. While this was done, they changed the DNA structure of the male and the female. But after a short time, unfavorable symptoms developed that alarmed Yokar. He took a sample of the female's signature and brought it to the One for her review. He mentioned to the One he noticed instead of feeling better and getting stronger; the opposite had happened.

Her suspicions got validated, and operations halted. She removed the Arcturian and Sirian geneticists. The One requested an assessment of the damage that had been done. The possibility existed they might have left genetic traps set to destroy the candidates. This concerned her the most.

She is now making it possible to restore their bodies by using an influx of thousands of millions of new stem cells to replace most of their entire body structure in the areas that were damaged. She told Yokar the approach was the safest way to remove potential traps.

While the stem cell therapy continued, the One instructed Yokar to watch their progress in this second phase. He confirmed the contaminated parts in their neural pathways were being eliminated and reconstruction of their original DNA was proceeding.

Then it was discovered as the quantity of stem cells was substantially increased, the quantity of foreign red blood cells already present were also increasing in the serum. Yokar determined that this effect contaminated the serum and would cause immune reactions and great stress for their liver to thwart those foreign blood cells in their bodies. This was brought to the laboratory's attention and the new serum was put through a unique filtering method, eliminating the red blood cell contamination. The therapy continues until the 'magic number' of cells is reached. The candidates are being made ready for the third phase, the merger.

The Kieralon male and female overshadow their human

counterparts and are making attempts at communication as the repair of their human bodies continues. When the stem cells get added after their repair is complete, the cells will accumulate into an "egg."

The One's energy is infused into every new cell after entry into the human body. The One will of the One will plan colonies of a higher vibration within the egg. An egg will grow and multiply within their human bodies until a singularity exists throughout their body and ignition can occur. Then they will avalanche into a spiritual chain reaction that will cause a higher frequency of singularity. This higher singularity frequency allows the Kieralon counterparts to merge with the human counterparts permanently. Then Phase four of the mission will be implemented.

With this accomplished, the third level capacity of the human counterparts provides prolonged staying power in the third dimension for the fifth level beings. Then it becomes possible for the fifth level Kieralon to enter the core of the Earth and retrieve the Nome-Lu-Lu. Once free and awakened, the Nome-Lu-Lu will merge their 7th level consciousness of the light worlds with the Kieralon / humans to make a triple hybrid. The phase four template for her new species will then be complete.

The One plans to bring this new hybrid species to a new Tiamat-like planet far away in a less turbulent area of the galaxy. From there, this new species will spread her way beyond the upper kingdom of the light worlds, into the middle kingdom of the astral worlds, and to the lower kingdom of the physical worlds. Once accomplished, all sentient life forms will experience the freedom of her way. The only caveat is the Djinn might construe her action as breaking the truce. But the Djinn have already broken the truce by their continued actions to support of Luxcius's revenge. Barring another war in heaven, the One Most High will have succeeded.

Epilogue

Given what we have said, circumstances within the loop make it impossible for those inside to escape from this reptilian preserve. This earth is a prison locked in a temporal loop designed and built by and for the Reptilians.

The Highest God intends to free the Nome-Lu-Lu that are locked within the invisible bubble of time. But the Highest God cannot sustain her existence in the lower realms for long and it is also true for the Kieralons. She will need to awaken the Nome-Lu-Lu and their crystalline forms will need to be shattered. She will need the surrogates from the Humans and Kieralons to help her with that.

For the Kieralons to can sustain the loop frequency, the higher vibrations of the Nome-Lu-Lu, and shatter the crystalline forms, require a great deal of energy and steadiness. Meanwhile, the two chosen Humans will have merged with their Kieralon counterparts. When their transformation is complete, then the two chosen humans will provide the steadiness the Kieralons need to complete their task.

By altering their vibrations, the Kieralons can penetrate the loop and seek the location of the Nome-Lu-Lu. Once the Kieralons awaken the Nome-Lu-Lu and shatter their crystalline cells, they will be free to allow the Kieralons to merge with them. The Kieralons will alter their vibrations along with the Nome-Lu-Lu to synchronize with the frequency of the loop. Then all three, the humans, the Kieralons and the Nome-Lu-Lu will leave the loop. After the extraction is complete, they will all join with the Highest God to function as a template for a new species in the quantum void, on a new earth and under a new sun.

The awful truth is the real Earth passed and almost all with it. Those who escaped in real time to colonize elsewhere in the galaxy before the catastrophe happened are aware of the catastrophe, but they are not aware of the loop's existence because it falls outside their perceived reality in another dimension.

The experience of those trapped is kept in the loop by the Reptilian's version of the reincarnation system operating inside the loop. It doesn't lead anyone on earth anywhere except back into the loop with no real spiritual progress other than what they have been told to believe. They are all in illusion about their spiritual development. Upon death, they will meet their loved ones at the portal to encourage them to re-enter for another new life without remembrance of the old one. Those that greet them are mere apparitions copied from their memories of those who have passed.

All the spiritual systems and spiritual training that goes on here in loop life are systems designed to keep the 'inmates' of the prison happy and cooperative by providing false hopes that their efforts promise a better life here and elsewhere.

The Highest God is allowing this to continue without interference until they destroy the loop and the human energy released.

The illusion from the prison is strong. Reptilian mind control wields power over the consciousness on Earth. It binds everyone daily to its apparent reality. Even those who govern are falsely told they are in charge. They behave as slave masters for the Reptilians' agenda, while their greed, avarice, cruel and violent behavior are encouraged along with their lies and deceit to the people to give them false security. Those that govern also feel the dark overlords favor them over the rest of the masses.

The illusion of hope for an afterlife call everyone to sleep, seducing them by its false comfort. Meanwhile, they infuse everyone's consciousness with violence, fear, and greed (survival mode) and encourage conflict and war as a solution to resolve their hate. The Reptilians know that strong hate only fosters more hate. All one must do is observe the Middle East and the conflicts in the Eastern block of Europe to see this. Then the Reptilians can feed from that energy like vampires.

On a final note, the remaining children of the fallen that escaped the earth catastrophe have moved on and continue to flourish in the outer regions of the solar system and in other star systems as space farers and traders, creating new human communities on other planets just like any other polarized life thriving in the galaxy.

The quantum void is not limited to or locked in a temporal loop. When the loop is destroyed, humanity's essence within the loop will release into the quantum.

The time ends this travesty, and that time is very near and held in the greatest and highest expectation by all who support her way in this or any other universe.

[Note to the reader): The Highest God requested that all

Epilogue

truth be revealed now! The truth is so shocking. There was tremendous difficulty to write it on paper. Then it was even more difficult to release it to the public.

The process of this divine task tests one's faith every day in every way. It forces one to deal with the fear of change and the sadness of being isolated from friends and family, and yet, they must endure all of that for her plan to truly succeed.

Glossary of Terms

Akasha (Indo–Aryan)
Aspect of the astral kingdom that exhibits a sticky or retentive quality; it is sensitive to all conscious vibrations from any sentient being and stores all experience in its infinite field of influence.

Akashic Record
Total record of the astral kingdom of sentient experience through all time and existence.

Channel
Psychically gifted person who exhibits communication with the elements and/or beings from other dimensions of reality other than the known three dimensional or physical world of Earth.

Djinn (pronounced "Gin")
Immortal beings and creator intelligences, emerging from the darkness of space as the race of Djinn, creatures existing outside time and space, which were part of existence before existence, as we know it, began.

Guide, Spirit
Spiritual friend or guardian in charge of teaching or assisting from the realm of spirit with the contracted embodied spirit (physical person) on Earth. Not to be confused with angels. Guardian angels—a misnomer—are also known as spirit guides.

Glossary of Terms

Lemur/Lemurian

Legendary animal creatures to host human consciousness (Stellar Mind) involving the first, second, and third root races of man; Lemurian relates to the fourth and final successful development of bipedal aquatic humanoids existing in a small region of the great continent of Gwandana, located in what is now the Pacific ocean.

Life Force

Primordial creative conscious and intelligent energy that springs from the origin of things, the building block of visible and invisible worlds. It flows around, permeates, and binds all living things together, containing male, female, and neutral components.

Most High/ Most High God/The One (Pre-diluvian)

Prime Creator God or Djinn; the first soul with free will, unconditional love, and compassion; Mother of all things in Her realm and the realm of Earth; divine immortal being from the race of Djinn, the first of Her kind.

Pan

Of legendary origin, pre-diluvian part man–part goat, demonstrating strong sexual connotations and images in mythology. According to pre-flood accounts, the Stellar Mind Pan led a rebellion during the third infusion of the Lemurian root race, and established a separate island colony of half-breeds and many different species near what is known as

Madagascar. Pan was part of the fall of spirit and repented and remained on Earth with his followers to serve the Most High God as caretaker of nature residing in the astral realm of Earth.

Solar Orb
Bright "hole" that appears as a fiery ball in space, allows the light of the high spirit realm to shine on Earth and solar system. Controlled by Askargon, the Solar Logoi.

Solar Logoi (Esoteric origin)
Conscious spiritual force or radiant intelligent energy believed to represent a pattern of spiritual development involving the transformation of fear, residing in the solar system and located in the body of the sun.

Soul (Hebrew origin)
Religious description of the element, or spark, of "God," living in a human being from birth, related to Jehovah, or Yahweh (Anunnaki deity), influencing human affairs.

Stellar Mind (Pre-diluvian)
Aspect of the triple mystery of the Most High God, defined as energy, form, and witness; an essence differing by qualities relating to the original matrix of the first loving soul out of the immortal Djinn.

Subtle Body (Esoteric origin)
Element making up the soul imprint, as of the structure of consciousness from the Stellar Mind aspects, various vibrational levels of spiritual existence, such as causal, etheric, mental, emotional and astral, which emerge into physical existence.

Tiamat/Earth (Pre-diluvian, Sumerian or Greek origin, Tellus)
Spirit integrated into living planet called Earth for transformation of the fallen Stellar Minds caught in the physical illusion and contraction of God consciousness.

www.ingramcontent.com/pod-product-compliance
Lightning Source LLC
Chambersburg PA
CBHW052018070526
44584CB00016B/1798